HOW TO STUDY

SECOND EDITION

David H. Griswold

WAYSIDE PUBLISHING

PRINTED IN THE UNITED STATES

ISBN 1-877653-51-9

CONTENTS

(continued)

"My Dog Ate It"

"My dog ate it."

"By mistake, I mailed it to my pen pal in Tennessee, and he forgot to mail it back to me."

"I put it in the pocket of my shirt, and my mom put the shirt through the wash."

"Someone stole it."

"It dropped out of my bag on the school bus."

"I don't need to do schoolwork. I'm the creative type."

"My computer didn't save it."

Excuses, excuses, excuses. . . .

You can blame it on your dog, on your pen pal, on someone else, on your mother, on the school bus, or even on the computer. But the plain fact is, excuses do not work very well.

Most teachers have heard them all. (The ones above, believe it or not, were used as "real" excuses.) Furthermore, students use excuses to take the blame from themselves and put it on fate or someone else. Although excuses may seem "real" to you, the fact is that you have not faced the situation and taken responsibility for doing what was asked of you.

Doing your work, and doing it on time, is precisely what this book is all about.

If you want to learn to study and don't know how, this book is for you.

Then you won't need to make up any excuses.

PREFACE TO THE SECOND EDITION

The second edition of *How to Study* has retained most of the basic design of the original edition, which students and teachers have said was so useful to them over the past ten years. The order of the units remains pretty much the same (with the exception of the inclusion of a new unit on stress), and the idea of presenting "easy" or "short" solutions at the beginning of each unit is still intact.

There are, however, four major additions to the book, most of them the result of changes in technology. First, throughout the text is advice to readers using computers. Second, computers have revolutionized libraries, and students are given guidance in how to use these computerized facilities.

Since these are days that demand speed and efficiency, they are days that often bring excessive stress, and so the third addition has been a short unit on managing stress. The final addition has been the inclusion of a useful new Appendix (III) that gives classroom teachers a clear way in which *How to Study* can be used with students in a structured, six-week program.

In helping me with their expert advice, I give thanks to Marcia Fosnot and Janice Lindberg. I am especially grateful to Mary Clark, Donna Santilla, Jules Spotts, and, of course, Anne Griswold for their extensive help and support in this undertaking.

Acknowledgments

Page 50, Longman Publishing Group for the reproduction of a page taken from *The French Revolution* by Gerald P. Dartford. Copyright © 1972.

Page 68, Zaner-Blowser for adaptation of material taken from an article entitled "Modality" by Walter B. Barbe and Michael N. Milone, Jr., which originally appeared in the January 1980 issue of *Instructor* magazine.

Page 98, Adapted from *The Relaxation and Stress Reduction Workbook* by Davis, Eshelman, and McKay, New Harbinger Publications, Oakland, Calif., 1988, as printed in *Studying for Success* by Lewis and O'Neill, Longman Chesire, Australia.

Pages 111–112, Definitions of terms adapted from *How to Study* by Clifford T. Morgan and James Deese. Copyright © 1969 by McGraw-Hill Book Company. Used with permission of the McGraw-Hill Book Company.

Page 133, "Signal Words" reprinted from *Study Skills: A Student's Guide for Survival* by Robert A. Carman and W. Royce Adams. Copyright © 1972 by John Wiley & Sons, Inc. Used by permission of the publisher.

Page 157, Excerpt from the *Readers' Guide to Periodical Literature.* Copyright © 1980 by the H.W. Wilson Company. Material reproduced with the permission of the publisher.

Page 166, Much of this material was taken from a handout and a letter used at the Trinity Preparatory School, Winter Park, Florida. Used with the kind permission of Donna Santilla, who devised the program.

GETTING STARTED

The beginning is the most
important part of . . . work.

                  Plato

[*NOTE:* Throughout this book, brackets are used to bring attention to suggestions that apply to students using computers.]

[*CAUTION:* Some schools or teachers may consider the use of the spell-check or the grammar-check a form of cheating and not permit their students to do so.]

1

Seven Shortcuts
to Using This Book

2

Five Ways You Can Use This Book to Help You

You are a unique person. As such, the ways in which you learn something are sometimes different from the ways in which others learn the same thing. Some learn quickly, some slowly. Some seem to learn by instinct; others have to work at it.

This is a unique book because it recognizes your individuality. The chapters are organized so that you can use them in the way that suits *you* best.

Here are five ways you can use this book:

1. You may read straight through from beginning to end.

2. You may diagnose your own particular studying problems on pages 11–13 and then use those sections that are most useful for you.

3. You may try a variety of techniques that suit your needs and your personality.

4. You may want to use only the "easy" methods placed at the beginning of each unit.

5. You may use a unit or a chapter within a unit as a self-contained section, without having to read previous pages.

Whatever approach you decide to take, you should give careful consideration to asking an advisor to help you (see page 5).

You should also read and understand the practical philosophy behind this book (pages 6–8).

3 *Should You Go the Study Route Alone?*

By looking into this book, you have already made one important decision: You need help in improving your study skills.

Before you go on, you have another important decision to make:

- Do you have the self-discipline to improve your study skills alone?

- Or do you need an advisor to help you?

This book is designed to be used either way. You should, however, give careful thought to asking an adult to help you, particularly if you tend to put things off, consider yourself poorly organized, or lack self-discipline.

If you plan to ask an adult to help you, here are some suggestions for choosing an advisor:

- Choose someone with enough time to spend with you *every day.*

- Choose someone with an interest in you *as a person.*

- Choose someone who you think is *well organized* and has *good judgment.*

After you have chosen your advisor, ask him or her to start by reading Appendixes I–IV on pages 159–168. Then take the diagnostic test on pages 11–13 and ask for help in following the recommendations on page 16.

If you plan to go it alone, you can start immediately by diagnosing your specific study problems on pages 11–13.

4

How to Go into Training

Beginning a new program of study is much like an athlete going into training. After making a commitment to a sport, an athlete must give up certain leisure-time pursuits and concentrate on doing a few simple things well.

Furthermore, in order to achieve mastery, athletes must practice again and again in those areas in which they are weak. If a tennis player, for example, has a poor backhand and yet wishes to become a good player, constant practice will be necessary to overcome the weakness.

You, too, must be prepared to give up some activities in order to master the study skills you lack. You, too, must practice until you have mastered your weaknesses.

The more skillful you become at studying, the more time you can spend later on pursuing those things you have had to give up temporarily. It is important to remember, also, that you may not be able to eliminate all your weaknesses, but at least you can learn how to *compensate* for them.

If you are serious about "going into training" for studying, here are some suggestions about ways to get started:

- Consider having an advisor—a teacher or another adult—who can help you every day.

- Draw up *on paper* [or on your computer] a list of objectives for yourself, and work on them *one at a time.* These objectives could include one or more of the following:
  - Improving a grade in one subject
  - Improving listening in class
  - Improving the efficient use of your time
  - Eliminating distractions
  - Learning the technique of good note-taking
  - Studying the text effectively

• Setting up a manageable homework schedule

• [Learning to type]

• [Learning to use a computer]

■ Make this initial list of objectives short. [You can use your computer for this list.] Work first on the weakness you think is most important to overcome. Then the next one. Do *not* try to do too many things at the same time since you could become overwhelmed and discouraged.

Suppose, for example, you set three goals for yourself. List them *in order* of importance to you.

• Do homework better

• [Learn to type]

• Improve listening in class

■ Next list the steps you feel you must take to reach your goals. (Ask your advisor for help, if you have one.)

Here is an example:

---

1. Do homework better: read Unit III, pages 35–64
   Set up homework schedule
   Study straight through an assignment/no breaks
   Be neat

2. Learn to type
   Get software program for computer
   Type notes for history

3. Improve listening in class
   Sit in front of class
   Have homework ready

■ Review your list of objectives *every day*. Find out which ones you neglected and *why*. Then take immediate steps to correct them.

Use whatever method works for you, and keep using it.

- Keep careful track of your progress. [Use your computer to keep track of your grades.] File your tests and quizzes in a manila folder, and concentrate your efforts on those courses in which your grades are dropping.
- Seek help from teachers in courses that are giving you trouble. Ask these teachers to make clear their expectations for good study habits.
- Be persistent. Do not give up trying even for one day.
- Be patient. Some study methods may take weeks to develop.
- Simplify your methods as much as possible.
- Get support from friends and family in meeting your goals.

■ When you have completed all your objectives, you might want to give yourself some kind of reward. (Your advisor can help you carry out your objectives and perhaps suggest a reward.)

5 Ten Short Ways to Improve Your Study Skills Immediately

If you have leafed through this book, you may have become discouraged by the time, thought, and self-discipline it takes to begin a new program of study. If, then, you are interested only in quick solutions, this brief chapter has been included for you.

Here are ten short ways to improve your studying immediately:

1. Write a brief daily schedule similar to the one below and *stick to it*. [This schedule is easy to type on your computer.]

SCHOOL	ROOM OR HOME STUDY
Period 1 Math class	5:30–6:15 Math homework
Period 2 English class	6:15–7:15 Dinner; relax
Period 3 Study period	7:15–8:00 Read English
Review history	
Period 4 History class	8:00–8:45 Write lab report
Period 5 French class	8:45–9:15 *Break*
Period 6 Study period	9:15–9:45 History
French homework	
Period 7 Chemistry class	9:45–10:05 French vocab

2. Schedule your study time for the hard courses during school hours so that you can get help from your teachers when you need it. If you have no study time at school, arrive early or stay late to get help.

3. Do *all* of your homework and hand it in on time.

4. Write your work neatly [or type on your computer]. Neat papers get better grades. [Use the spell-check on your computer, but proofread carefully for problem words such as *form/from* and th*ere*/th*eir*/th*ey're*.]

5. Make sure all your work is *accurate* and *complete:*

   ▪ Show all steps in math problems and on lab reports.

   ▪ Spell and punctuate properly on all work to be handed in. [Use a spell-check, if permitted.]

   ▪ Keep an accurate, orderly notebook.

6. Write brief outlines for essays, themes, and compositions to be certain your writing assignments are well organized. [Use a computer to write outlines.]

7. Study when you say you are going to study.

8. Ask advice from your teachers about problems you are having *and do exactly what they suggest.*

9. Listen closely and look interested in the classroom. Participate actively in class discussions. Volunteer information you know for certain. Teachers like to see students putting forth good effort.

10. Be persistent. Keep at it every day.

If the above suggestions do not meet your needs, turn the page and take a diagnostic test to learn where you need help most.

6 *How to Diagnose Your Study Problems*

The self-administered test below is designed so that you can discover where your most serious study problems are.

After you have taken the test, turn to page 16 for specific ways in which you can help yourself to correct those problems.

	YES	NO
1. Do you know how much time you *really* spend studying?	_____	_____
2. Do you usually work when you say you will?	_____	_____
3. Do you know your best study time?	_____	_____
4. Do you have a workable, written study schedule that you follow every day?	_____	_____
5. Do you have a way to catch up on your homework when you fall behind?	_____	_____
6. Do you have a systematic way to do your homework every day?	_____	_____
7. Are your papers and your desk organized?	_____	_____
8. Is your notebook organized?	_____	_____
9. Do you have a useful system of note-taking?	_____	_____
10. Do you know how to outline or underline the text properly?	_____	_____

(*continued*)

	YES	NO
11. Do you know how a textbook can provide you with quick answers?	_____	_____
12. Do you know the most effective way to read a textbook?	_____	_____
13. Do you know how to make difficult ideas understandable?	_____	_____
14. Do you know what kind of learner you are?	_____	_____
15. Do you have good powers of concentration?	_____	_____
16. Do you have a good system for taking class notes?	_____	_____
17. Do you do well in courses where the teacher is disorganized or boring?	_____	_____
18. Do you know how to help yourself if you are "snowed under" with work?	_____	_____
19. Do you know how to manage excessive stress in and out of school?	_____	_____
20. Do you have a useful system for memorizing?	_____	_____
21. Do you have an efficient system for studying for quizzes, tests, and exams?	_____	_____
22. Do you usually finish a test on time?	_____	_____
23. Do you know how to avoid cramming at the last minute for exams?	_____	_____
24. Do you know how to avoid making careless mistakes on tests?	_____	_____

	YES	NO

25. Do you know how to remember where you put important school items? _____ _____

26. Do you read different material at different speeds? _____ _____

27. Do you have a program to improve your spelling? _____ _____

28. Do you have a program to expand your vocabulary? _____ _____

29. Do you know how to use the school library to improve your coursework? _____ _____

30. Can you easily locate what you need in the library? _____ _____

After you have finished filling in all the items, turn to page 16 for the best way to use the results of this test.

1

How to Recognize a Good Student

While it is difficult to classify all the qualities of a student having good study habits, some traits seem obvious. How well do you measure up to these traits?

The student having good study habits:

- Is a diligent, self-disciplined worker who has high academic standards and enjoys the challenges of schoolwork.
- Knows how to compensate for weaknesses. Hence, no two students study exactly alike:
  - Some learn largely by listening closely in class. Their recall is based chiefly on good note-taking.
  - Some rely heavily on note-taking from the text, abstracting material they know to be important.
  - Some (especially poor note-takers) rely on underlining the text and on frequent exposure to that underlining, usually three to six times before a test or quiz.
- Is a careful "teacher-watcher" and an excellent listener.
- Works according to a perception of what the teacher has stressed in class and judgment of the kinds of questions the teacher has asked on previous tests.
- Examines carefully all returned papers for clues as to where he or she went astray and takes steps not to make the same mistake twice.
- Is well organized and knows the logic and terminology of all the subjects being studied.
- Has an empathetic feel for the subject: knows the key questions the subject deals with, understands the discipline the subject requires, and is willing to take occasional risks.
- [Takes time to prevent errors by using the spell-check on the computer and then proofreading carefully. *CAUTION*: Some schools or teachers may not permit their students to use the spell-check or the grammar-check. Ask your teacher.]

8 *How to Recognize a Poor Student*

Like the good student, the poor student has some obvious traits. How many of these traits apply to you?

The student having poor study habits:

- Sets low goals, if any—or plays the grade game, just skimming by to keep parents and teachers from being an annoyance.

- Gives social life or sports too high a priority so that academic life suffers.

- Does not know how to compensate for weaknesses.

- Is often lost in the material of the course and cannot distinguish the important from the trivial.

- Has a poor span of concentration, does not listen closely in class, and does not take good notes, if any.

- Is confused by the subject itself, thinking that by its nature the subject is confusing and complicated, and that there is little that can be done to master the material.

- Is haphazard and disorganized in keeping to a daily or weekly study schedule.

- Looks at the material only superficially, usually only once.

- Has little concept of how the course or the text is organized.

- Thinks poorly of his or her own ability to do anything well at school.

9

How to Use the Results of Your Diagnostic Test

If you have answered *NO* to any of questions 1–5, turn to Unit II, pages 17–31.

If you have answered *NO* to any of questions 6–14, turn to Unit III, pages 33–64.

If you have answered *NO* to any of questions 15–18, turn to Unit IV, pages 65–88.

If you have answered *NO* to question 19, turn to Unit V, pages 89–98.

If you have answered *NO* to any of questions 20–23, turn to Unit VI, pages 99–114.

If you have answered *NO* to either question 24 or 25, turn to Unit VII, pages 115–124.

If you have answered *NO* to any of questions 26–28, turn to Unit VIII, pages 125–142.

If you have answered *NO* to either question 29 or 30, turn to Unit IX, pages 143–158.

UNIT II

TIME

Lost time is never found
again.

Benjamin Franklin

DO YOU WANT TO KNOW . . .   *TURN TO PAGE . . .*

1 *Three Easy Ways to Use Your Time Efficiently*

If you are an inefficient user of time and want some quick suggestions, here they are:

1. Develop a rhythm for studying. Early each day, draw up a quick schedule for doing your work. *Stick to it.*

   Here is a model of a brief daily schedule [that may be done on your computer]:

Before school—French
Per. 5–Study period   Math
5:00–5:45   Bio
ROOM STUDY
7:00–8:00   Read novel
8:00–9:00   History
9:00–9:15   Break
9:15–9:45   Review French

2. Do *not* put off things. Study when you say you are going to study. Do not become sidetracked by a friend, roommate, or any diversion. If you do become sidetracked, you *must* make up the lost time later in the day.

3. Plan your time to include relaxation. Give yourself something pleasurable to look forward to after you have finished studying and have completed all assignments.

2 How Much Time Do You Really *Spend Studying?*

It is only human to allow ourselves time for the things we *want* to do. However, if you are like most people, you may have difficulty planning time for the things you *have* to do. Striking a sensible balance between your personal needs and your academic demands is the key to efficient management of time.

Successful students, busy as they are, always seem to have enough time for activities both in school and elsewhere. Poor students, however, often seem pressed for time, or they use time in unproductive ways.

One way to begin a successful method of managing your time well is to have a *realistic* view of how much time you actually spend studying your subjects.

You may *think* you are spending a lot of time studying. If you want an accurate account of your management of time, fill in the chart below for *one full school day.*

Use minutes on the chart, not parts of hours.

Do *not* include time spent daydreaming, taking out books, getting organized. Fill in just the time spent *actually* studying.

Be honest with yourself.

Time spent studying	Math	English	Science	Language	Social Studies	Total

After you have filled out your chart for *one full day,* you may be able to draw some conclusions about the time spent and the retention you are likely to have. Compare the numbers in your chart to the chart below:

Total time spent in one day	Average minutes per course (5 courses)	Your retention is likely to be
75 min. or less	15 min. or less	Very poor
100 min. or less	20 min. or less	Weak
125 min. or less	25 min. or less	Only fair
150 min. or less	30 min. or less	Fair to good
200 min. or less	40 min. or less	Good

The chart above is intended only as a guideline to the actual amount of time you have spent studying. If you are putting in thirty to forty minutes a day on a course and are still having difficulty, there are two explanations: First, you may not be spending enough time on that course; second, you may be using inefficient methods of attacking the material.

On the other hand, a twenty-minute review session memorizing vocabulary, for example, may strengthen your comprehension significantly. Although there *is* a correlation between time spent and retention, the way in which you approach the material is equally important.

3 *How to Avoid Putting Things Off*

"I'm going to stop putting things off—starting tomorrow," goes the current saying. Procrastination is universal and often involves some kind of *rationalization* (that is, making up excuses to fit the reason). Here are some typical examples of rationalizing procrastination:

> "I'll do it later when I feel better."

> "I'll do the assignment after class so that I can understand the material better."

> "Instead of doing my assignment now, I'll do it tomorrow when I'm not as busy."

> "I don't see why I have to learn such-and-such anyway. When will it be useful to me?"

> "I can't face schoolwork now. I have too much on my mind."

Such rationalizing inevitably leads to leaving things undone that you *know* should be done. The result, of course, is that you risk falling further and further behind in your work. Instead of developing mastery of and confidence in the material, you may become the victim of it. You are, in fact, creating your own stress.

Moreover, you know better than anyone else that no one can *make* you stop procrastinating. Not this book, not your teachers, not anyone. The only one you can look to is yourself.

The answer to procrastination is an easy one: "Do it now!" But it is not always easy to put that into practice. The three following plans, then, are suggested ways of avoiding procrastination *if* you are serious about getting things done:

Plan 1

1. List in two columns all the things you have to do. Label *NOW* the most pressing ones. Label *LATER* the ones that can be put off for a short time. [You can do this on your computer.]
   Here is a sample list:

NOW	LATER
Make up English reading	Write lab report for Fri.
Correct math test	Begin research for hist. paper
Read history assignment	French vocab quiz Thurs.

2. Carry through *immediately* the items on your *NOW* list.

3. Begin to schedule *specific times* for your *LATER* activities as soon as you have finished your *NOW* list. *Do them when you say you will.*

Plan 2

1. Write a brief schedule for today, putting the most pressing items first. [You can do this on your computer.]
   Here is a sample list:

Before school	Make up Eng. homework
Period 5	Read history
5:30–6:15	Begin to write lab report for Fri.
7:30–8:00	Begin research for hist. paper

2. Follow your schedule *exactly as written.*

3. Draw up such a list early every day and *follow it exactly.*

Plan 3

(For especially long assignments such as a term paper.)

1. Break up the work into manageable segments of time of about thirty to forty-five minutes each.

2. List the steps and estimate the number of time segments needed for each step. [Most of this work can be done on a computer.] Here is a sample list:

> **HISTORY TERM PAPER**
> Gather material—3 periods
> Read and take notes—6 periods
> Outline material—2 periods
> Type draft—3 periods
> Edit draft—1 period
> Proofread final draft—1 period

3. Enter the steps on a schedule or calendar like the one below and keep it handy in your notebook:

	Mon	Tues	Wed	Thurs	Fri	Sat	Sun
Week 1	Gather material		Read and take notes				
Week 2	Outline/draft			Edit draft Proofread	Paper due		

4. As you start to work, try to save as much time as you can in the early stages so that you will not feel the pressure of a lot of work in the last few days.

4

When Is the Best Time for You to Study?

Scheduling your study time depends partly on knowing yourself and partly on common sense. If you consider your own patterns of alertness, you can discover those parts of the day in which you feel most alert:

- Some people are "day" people. That is, their powers of concentration are best suited to working during the day.

- Others are "night" people whose powers of concentration reach their peak at night.

- Some people are most alert in the morning. For others, late morning is the ideal time to concentrate.

- The times *least* suited to heavy concentration are before meals, after strenuous exercise, and just before bed.

If you know that fatigue is the enemy of concentration, you can exercise a little common sense on when to study.

Here are four suggestions as to the best times for you to study:

1. Schedule your most difficult subject first or when you feel most rested. (However, some students like to do their easy subjects first in order to get into the rhythm of studying.)

2. Do not try to study very difficult material for long stretches of time. If you have not completed the material in forty to sixty minutes, return to it later when you are feeling fresher.

3. Take a short break when your mind can absorb no more. Do *not* read. Instead, relax by taking a short walk or doing some physical exercise. (You might want to try a relaxation exercise. See page 98.)

4. Get enough sleep.

5

How to Schedule Your Study Time

Scheduling study time is a very personal matter that depends on many factors: your schedule of classes, your personal activities, your school commitments outside of class, and factors often beyond your control (such as having to catch up in one or more subjects because of absence or illness).

To make the best use of your time, you should think in terms of a monthly calendar as well as a weekly schedule.

Monthly calendar. Fill out a monthly calendar like the one on page 28. Include all major commitments of time *including personal ones.* Ask your teachers and parents to give you all important dates. Keep this calendar posted on the wall in front of your desk or placed in the front of your notebook.

Weekly schedule. Now draw up a weekly schedule like the one on page 29. Be sure to work around those time commitments on your monthly calendar.

Here are some guidelines for weekly scheduling:

- Study difficult subjects in small segments of twenty-five to thirty minutes each. *Two twenty-five-minute sessions of study are much better for retention than is one fifty-minute session.*

- Remove all distractions when you study. Clear your desk of anything that might keep you from working. Find the quietest place to study that you can.

- Schedule the subjects you have most difficulty in during school so that you can get help from your teachers or from fellow students.

- Schedule every subject *every day,* even if you do not have a class in that subject. A daily fifteen-minute review of the material will help your retention enormously.

- Schedule a review sometime during the weekend, preferably on Sunday afternoon or evening. A review of each subject will help your retention greatly. [This weekly schedule may be done on your computer.]

Review the schedule after one week; then draw up a new schedule based on your need for change. Keep copies of your schedule in the front of your notebook and in front of your desk.

If scheduling problems persist, consult a teacher, a well-organized friend, or your advisor.

If it is a matter of procrastination, see pages 22–24.

SUNDAY	MONDAY	TUESDAY	WEDNESDAY	THURSDAY	FRIDAY	SATURDAY
	OCTOBER			1	2	3
4	5 Dinner & show in city	6	7	8 Paper due in English	9	10
11	12 Columbus Day	13	14 12:00 – 5:00 Biology Field Trip	15	16	17
18	19	20	21 Aunt Minnie's Birthday Party	22	23	24 Camping weekend →
25	26	27 History paper due	28	29	30 Soccer trip 12:15	31

NAME:

WEEKLY STUDY SCHEDULE

TIME	MONDAY	TUESDAY	WEDNESDAY	THURSDAY	FRIDAY
S C H O O L					
S T U D Y					WEEKEND
TIME					
R O O M					
S T U D Y					

6 How to Catch Up if You Are Behind

If you have had to miss classes for a few days or more, it is essential that you make up the work. Your problem will be complicated by having to keep up with the current work as well as having to catch up on the work you missed. However, by determination and by the use of a few shortcuts, you can solve your problem in a few days.

Here are some steps you can take to help you make up for lost time:

- See each teacher and ask how best to make up the work you have missed.

- Borrow the class notes of a reliable student, but copy *only* what you need. [A good way to review the material is by typing notes on your computer.]

- Review the textbook by reading all headings in large black type. Note those sections that seem especially difficult and read them carefully.

- Draw up a temporary catch-up schedule, and attach it to your weekly schedule (see page 29). This schedule should be based on the following:
  - First priority: those tests and quizzes you have missed that have to be made up as quickly as possible.
  - Second priority: major projects you have fallen behind on that require teacher assistance.
  - All other daily work.

- Listen closely in class when a teacher says that material is important. Review such material in the text *thoroughly.*

- Ask questions in class on material that you have missed. If the teacher says that the material has already been covered and is reluctant to go over it again, schedule a conference and ask for an explanation of the material you are having problems understanding.

- If you are hopelessly behind in a course such as history, go to the library and get short, simplified versions of the material you missed.

- Make certain each teacher knows *exactly* what you have done and how much time you have spent in catching up.

UNIT III

HOMEWORK

It's what you do with a thing
that counts.

Robert Frost

DO YOU WANT TO KNOW . . .   *TURN TO PAGE . . .*

33

1 Six Short Ways to Do Your Homework Well

If you need quick solutions to the problems of homework, follow these suggestions:

- Write down your homework assignments *in the same place every day.* It is best to have a homework assignment sheet like the one on page 36.

- Do your homework in the same place every day—somewhere that is *quiet* and has *no distractions.*

- Plan your study schedule early in the day before classes begin. Study hard or boring subjects first.

- Do *not* procrastinate. Study straight through an assignment without interruption. However, do not study a hard subject for more than forty-five minutes. Schedule short breaks between subjects.

- Make certain you have done *everything* the assignment requires.

- Write *neatly* or type all of your work to be handed in. [Use the spell-check and grammar-check on papers you hand in.]

SAMPLE HOMEWORK ASSIGNMENT SHEET

	Monday Date:	Tuesday Date:	Wednesday Date:	Thursday Date:	Friday Date:
Math					
French					
English					
History					
Science					
Other					

2 *How to Make Studying Work for You*

Your chief aim in developing any study program should be to bring the demands of school into harmony with your individuality and personality. To this end, your guiding principle should be: *Use whatever techniques work best for you and keep using them.*

The principles that guide an athlete bent on self-improvement should be the same as those that guide a successful study program:

Capitalize on your strengths.

Compensate for your weaknesses.

Here are some guidelines to keep in mind as you develop your program of studying:

Never rely solely on memory. You may *think* you can recall what was said in class, but studies have proved that only about 25 percent of what was said in class can be recalled with accuracy, and then for only a short period of time. So, if you want to remember it, *write it down.*

Never dwell upon past mistakes or failures. Look over corrected papers carefully with the idea of *learning* from your mistakes. Do *not* think, "How stupid I am." Instead, think, "The next time I should. . . . "

Always set goals for yourself that you can achieve. Do *not* compare yourself to habitually successful students. Do *not* keep blaming teachers for your setbacks. *Do* reward yourself for a job well done.

Always keep a brief, accurate record of your grades in the front of your notebook [or in your computer]. Progress may not always come easily or quickly, but remember that *any* progress is better than none.

7

Four Proven Ways to Do Your Homework

Doing homework can be one of the most boring and difficult tasks a student has to face. Since it is usually the only school task one has to do by oneself, a student must come to grips with both the self-discipline and loneliness that go with homework.

If you need motivation, you can make a game of it in these ways:

- You can say to yourself, "After I have finished my Latin and math, I will treat myself to such-and-such."

- For variety, you can change the order in which you usually study your subjects.

- You can try setting up a specific time to complete each subject and try to keep within the time you have set.

The problems of homework can involve many different approaches. Since some of the suggestions below may be contradictory, feel free to adapt them to your needs.

Here are four proven ways to do your homework:

1. *Know where to study*

Study at the quietest place in school for subjects requiring maximum concentration.

Study at your desk, not lying on your bed.

Where there are unavoidable distractions, do only the work requiring the least concentration.

For a test review—or for subjects in which you are struggling—study with fellow students.

2. *Make a plan of study*

Make a daily study schedule early in the day based on your monthly calendar (see page 28).

Anticipate important tests. Begin to study for major tests at least *three days* ahead of time.

Anticipate important papers. Begin researching and organizing important papers *at least a week or ten days* ahead of time.

3. Decide the order in which to study _____

Study hard subjects first.

Study boring subjects first.

Do right/wrong, noninterpretive subjects first: math, science, language, for example.

Always review your class notes from that day before studying new material.

4. Keep your concentration _____

Never break your concentration in the middle of an assignment.

Never mix subjects together in a short span of time, say twenty or thirty minutes.

Take a short break after studying for an hour.

Never play the radio or stereo or watch TV during demanding assignments.

Read important material two or three times for maximum retention.

Avoid procrastinating. Do *not* give in to the temptation to [play a computer game or] phone a friend.

4 *How to Organize Your Desk*

As the demands of schoolwork become more pressing, students' desks tend to become more cluttered. It is therefore important to keep an orderly desk so as not to risk the loss or misplacement of important papers and books.

Your desk should be:

- A place for paper, pens, and pencils.

- [A place for your computer and printer.]

- A place for filing papers [and storing computer disks].

- A place for reference books and textbooks [as well as computer manuals].

Here are some suggestions to help you organize your desk.

- Remove from your desk anything that clutters or gets in the way of studying: magazines, trophies, hobbies, letters, etc.

- Make certain that the desk is not facing a distraction like a window.

- Make sure that your desk lamp gives good light.

- Get an adjustable office chair for those long writing assignments.

- Organize the space in your desk and its compartments so that you can easily lay your hands on anything you need.

Here is a typical well-organized desk:

- Pencils, pens, sharpeners, etc., are in a plastic organizer on the top of the desk. (Using drawers for pencils, pens, etc., just wastes time.)

- The only books on top of the desk are textbooks, reference books (such as dictionaries), and any books you need for studying your particular assignment.

- Drawers are organized for quick and easy access to papers:
    - Extra supplies are stored in the top drawer.
    - Tests and papers are filed in one drawer.
    - Personal papers are put away in another drawer.

- Most important, neither the top of the desk nor the drawers have any material that is not important or usable.

- The monthly calendar and homework assignments for the day or week are posted on the wall in front of the desk.

5

How to Organize Your Papers

Corrected papers can be a tremendous help in improving your grades by signaling where you went wrong and suggesting what you might do to correct your errors. Keep in mind the analogy between yourself improving your grades and an athlete who wants to do better:

Take advantage of your strengths.

Work to correct your weaknesses.

Throwing away or ignoring corrected papers after they have been returned to you is throwing away important and useful information. Since corrected papers indicate a teacher's judgment of where your weaknesses are, you must develop a filing system that makes it easy to retrieve these papers.

Remember: Use any system that works for you, but keep it simple. Here are some suggestions for setting up an efficient filing system:

- Keep in your notebook those papers that are *immediately* useful. As soon as they have outlived their usefulness, file them in manila folders or throw them away. Weed out your notebook once a week.

- Save corrected homework papers until after comprehensive tests or exams. Then throw them away.

- Save all important quizzes, tests, and exams.

- File papers in manila folders by subject. Clip papers together by date—most recent on top.

- Go through the files every week or so and weed out any papers that are no longer useful.

- File papers *upright* in the drawer so that you do not have to remove stacks of folders to get to the one you want.

- Keep all filed papers in the *same* drawer in your desk so that you will not have to hunt around for an important paper.

- [Use a backup system on your computer to save important notes and other material.]

6 *How to Organize Your Notes*

A good set of organized notes is indispensable to success at school. Good notes have two advantages: They order material, and they help you to retain important information.

Think of your notes as a computer: You feed in information and retrieve it when you need it. The better organized your notes are, the easier it is to retrieve what you need.

There are two systems of organizing notes, each with advantages and disadvantages:

1. The three-ring binder method. This system has the advantage of having *all* your notes together in a single notebook. Since your notes are all clipped together, they are accessible for all your classes, and it is easy to remember to take them with you. The major disadvantage is, if you lose your notebook you lose everything. In spite of this disadvantage, the three-ring-binder method is probably a better system than the use of separate notebooks.

2. Separate notebooks for each course. This system has the advantage of relative safety. If you lose a notebook for one course, the rest are safe. However, it has distinct disadvantages: Separate notebooks tend to become scattered among classrooms, study area, homeroom, and library. Furthermore, students sometimes find that they have brought the wrong notebook to class. If you like to use separate notebooks, use them for things like vocabulary lists or notes that can be easily copied if the book is lost. [If you store notes in your computer, use a backup system in anticipation of a power failure.]

Remember: Use any system that works for you, but keep it simple and manageable.

Since the three-ring binder is the more useful system, the following suggestions apply chiefly to that method.

Here is how to organize a three-ring binder:

- Get a set of dividers and label them with the course names.

- Place each labeled divider in the order in which the course occurs in your daily schedule.

- Keep a copy of your homework assignments and weekly study schedule *in the front* of your notebook on the left side.

- Place your uncorrected homework papers *in the same place* every day. Students generally keep such papers in one of three places: (1) in the front of the notebook, on the right side, (2) in the back of the notebook, in a pocket, or (3) in the front section of each subject.

- File important papers by subject. Do not put uncorrected and corrected papers in the same place.

- Keep all papers flat and clipped in the notebook. Loose papers can drop out, tear, or become lost.

- Weed out your notebook at least once a week. Less current papers should be filed in the manila folders in your desk. All unimportant papers should be thrown away.

- Write on both sides of the paper when taking notes in class (see pages 76–78). Use the right-hand side for outlining and study notes and the left-hand side for class notes.

- Keep all important class handouts in the front of each section of each subject.

- Buy a new notebook if the back breaks or if the cover comes off. Broken binders are a risk to the safekeeping of your important notes.

7 How to Decide Which Method of Note-Taking to Use

There are three methods of taking notes from books, each having advantages and disadvantages. You should know the pros and cons of each method and then adapt the one that best suits you and the material you are studying.

Here are the advantages and disadvantages of each method, and the type of material best suited to each method:

Underlining (or highlighting) alone

Advantages:

Speed and accuracy.

Convenience of always having information in the same place—in the book itself.

Disadvantages

Cannot be done unless student owns book.

A passive, not an active, method of note-taking.

Retention of material likely to be weak.

A tendency to underline too much or too little.

A tendency to underline the wrong things.

Difficulty in reviewing for exams: too much material.

Material best suited for underlining or highlighting:

Important passages in literature: novels, plays poetry.

Most textbooks: history, social sciences, some science.

See pages 48–51 for a method of underlining alone.

Outlining alone

Advantages:

Material is ordered and condensed.

An active, not a passive, method of note-taking.

Class notes face outline from the book.

Recall of material is likely to be better than using underlining alone.

[Can be typed on (and saved by) your computer.]

Disadvantages:

More time-consuming than underlining alone.

Outlined material may not always be accurate.

Tendency not to review outlined material enough.

Material best suited for outlining alone:

Plots of plays, chapters from novels.

Most textbooks: history, social sciences, some science.

See pages 52–56 for a method of outlining alone.

Underlining (or highlighting) and outlining

Advantages:

Combines the best features of both methods.

Material is ordered and condensed.

Frees student from having to refer to the book often.

Recall of material is likely to be excellent.

Disadvantages:

Most time-consuming form of note-taking.

Demands most self-discipline to perfect.

Material best suited for underlining and outlining:

Most textbooks: history, social sciences, some science.

See pages 48–56 for methods of underlining and outlining.

8

How to Underline (or Highlight) the Textbook

Underlining (or highlighting) the text is a popular method of studying because it offers both speed and accuracy. There are, however, major pitfalls in using only underlining, the most important one being that many students fail to go back and study the passages they have underlined.

There are other drawbacks to using only underlining as well:

- Students who do not own their own texts are asked not to underline.

- It is a passive, not an active, method of note-taking. That is, the only work you do is to draw lines; you do not process the information in your own words.

- Underlining always raises the question, "What is important to underline?" As a result, some students underline too much because they are afraid of missing the major points. Other students seem to underline the wrong things, missing many important ideas.

- Underlining can be helpful on weekly tests, but studying great quantities of underlined passages for an examination can be frustrating and overwhelming.

- Underlining often gives students a false sense of security. They feel that they have done the assignment if they have underlined carefully and, as noted above, seldom return to review the underlined passages.

If you feel, however, that underlining by itself is the best study method for you, here are some guidelines to follow:

- Decide in advance exactly what you want to underline. Turn to the questions at the end of each section or chapter and underline *only* the answers to those questions.

- Listen closely in class for the points the teacher stresses. *Keep your book open* during class and check to see if you have underlined those points. If you have not, underline points stressed in class in a different color from the one you used for your homework. Then, the next time you study, try to figure out *why* you missed those important points.

- Review your underlining carefully immediately after you have completed it and again before class begins.

- Review *all* underlining again after a week's work.

- Check with a fellow student who is doing well in the course to see where you have gone astray.

- In your class notes, write down the page numbers of important underlined passages. When you study for a test, keep both underlining and class notes in front of you.

- Take complete and accurate class notes to clarify or expand on ideas.

- Keep your underlining *simple:* The only *complete* sentences you should underline are usually the *topic sentences* of paragraphs. (Topic sentences announce the main idea of a paragraph and are usually the first sentence.)

- Underline only essential information within each sentence. Exclude all nonessential information.

- Use the same underlining method for class notes and outlining notes (see pages 52–56).

On the next page is an example of underlining from the opening chapter of a book on the French Revolution:

CHAPTER 1

THE COLLAPSE OF DESPOTISM

(1) The Decline of the French Monarchy

During the summer of 1789 Louis XVI, heir to the greatest monarchy in Europe, decided to call the States General of France, which had not met for 175 years. The king and his advisers intended that this medieval parliament[1] should deal with certain specific matters referred to it by the Crown, as it had always done in the past. At this time the most urgent problem was the grave financial crisis that had reduced the French government to bankruptcy. In fact the meeting of the States General in May 1789 opened the floodgates of change and marked the beginning of the French Revolution.

During the century preceding this event, there had been a steady decline in the efficiency and prestige of the monarchy in France. Three kings occupied the throne during these hundred years. Louis XIV (1643–1715) had built up the machinery of despotic rule, and no one had ever acted the part of an absolute monarch more magnificently. At the peak of his success in the 1680s Louis XIV had raised France to an almost unquestioned ascendancy politically and culturally in Europe. The French army, remodeled by Louvois, the war minister, and led by Turenne, Condé, and Vauban, the greatest generals of their age, had enjoyed more than forty years of unbroken victory. Military might was backed by a skillful and active diplomacy. The prestige of France was extended through Europe and as far as Siam in distant Asia.

Within the French kingdom, this success had been made possible by the reforms of the finance minister, Colbert, and the encouragement he gave to the building of roads and canals, the development of industry and commerce, and the increase of the French navy and mercantile marine. French writers, artists, architects, and musicians set the fashion for a culture that was admired and copied in every capital from London to Moscow.

Topic sentence

Topic sentence

Topic sentence

1. The States General was the nearest equivalent to a legislature or parliament in the English sense. The French *parlements* were appeals courts, not legislatures.

Please note the following:

- The chapter title and the main heading have both been underlined twice.

- Two of the three topic sentences have been underlined completely.

- Only essential points in other sentences have been underlined: important supporting details, important names, and dates.

- Even the essential detail in the footnote has been underlined.

9 How to Outline from the Textbook

Outlining is more demanding and time-consuming than underlining alone, yet it is more useful. Outlining offers the advantages of better recall than just underlining and is a more ordered and condensed way of seeing the material. Outlining used in conjunction with underlining is more effective yet.

Your notes should serve the same function as a computer: Accurate material is fed in and is retrieved easily when needed. Outlining is best used for factual data in courses such as history and the social sciences. Outlining cannot be used for most math courses and beginning language courses.

The purpose of outlining is to free you, as much as possible, from having to rely on the textbook. If you have good outline notes and good class notes, you can study more quickly and effectively for tests and exams.

Here are some guidelines regarding outlining:

Outlining should *condense* and *simplify* textual material.

Outlining should be *consistent* in style and should *order* the material according to importance.

Outlining should be reviewed *immediately* after taking notes, again as soon as possible before class, and again at least once a week thereafter.

Outlining should be written on the *right-hand* side of the notebook, leaving the left-hand side for class notes.

Outlining should *not* be long and cumbersome. Too many notes are often as bad as too few.

[Typing the outline on your computer can give you three advantages. It helps you memorize the material better. It is easy to revise and to reorder items. And it is neat and easy to read when reviewing.]

Here are the eight steps in outlining:

1. Decide first what you plan to outline. You can make your decision based on three things: the points the teacher has stressed in class; the questions at the end of the chapter or section; and the organization of the book in chapters, headings, and sub-headings.

2. Skim briefly through the text, reading everything in large black print so that you can see what topics are covered in the assignment and in what order.

3. (Include this step *only* if you plan to underline or highlight and then take notes.) Underline the material according to the three suggestions in Step 1. Underline the topic sentence of each paragraph (the sentence containing the main idea). Also underline supporting detail, but only for important words and phrases that are used to support the main ideas. (See pages 76–78 for a fuller discussion of outlining.)

4. Take notes as you read. Note the way in which the text is organized. Copy chapter titles and headings word for word, although headings can be abbreviated. Use this form:

CHAPTER TITLE (top of page)

I.   MAIN HEADING OR IDEA (preceded by a Roman numeral)
    A.   SUPPORTING DETAIL #1 (preceded by a capital letter)
    B.   SUPPORTING DETAIL #2 (preceded by a capital letter)
    C.   SUPPORTING DETAIL #3 (preceded by a capital letter)
       1.   SUBDETAIL #1 (preceded by a number)
       2.   SUBDETAIL #2 (preceded by a number)
II.   MAIN HEADING OR IDEA (preceded by a Roman numeral)
    A.
    B.
    C.

5. Write in telegraphic style and abbreviate. Telegraphic style leaves out all articles (*a, an, the*) and unimportant verbs (*is, can, be, went,* etc.). Develop your own system of abbreviations by using symbols, apostrophes, and abbreviated endings. Here are a few examples of abbreviations:

$$
\begin{aligned}
\text{ch(s)} &= \text{chapter(s)} \\
\text{p} &= \text{page} \\
\text{pp} &= \text{pages} \\
\& &= \text{and} \\
@ &= \text{at} \\
\text{b/c} &= \text{because} \\
\text{vs} &= \text{versus, as opposed to} \\
\text{pol} &= \text{politics or political} \\
\text{prob} &= \text{problem} \\
\text{w/} &= \text{with} \\
\text{w/o} &= \text{without} \\
\text{govt} &= \text{government} \\
\text{Pres} &= \text{President} \\
\text{acc to} &= \text{according to} \\
\text{Reps} &= \text{Representatives} \\
\text{fr} &= \text{from} \\
\text{ea} &= \text{each} \\
\text{syst} &= \text{system} \\
\text{VP} &= \text{Vice-President}
\end{aligned}
$$

You should remember two things about using abbreviations:

- Spell out the name of an abbreviated form the first time you come to it (for example, "World Health Organization"). The next time you use it, you can abbreviate ("WHO," for example).

- Keep your abbreviations consistent. For example, if you use *ind,* you may not know in reviewing your notes whether it stands for *independent, individual,* or *indirect.* In this case, extend your abbreviation to five or more letters: *indep* for *independent, indiv* for *individual,* and *indir* for *indirect.*

Here is a brief example of an outline showing the three branches of the government as given in the Constitution:

U.S. CONSTITUTION (Chapter Title)

I. U.S. Pol Syst = 3 branches   (Section Heading—Main Idea)
   A. Legislative (Congress): makes laws   (Subheading)
      1. Senate—100 mems—2 fr ea state   (Supporting detail)
      2. House of Reps—435 mems—acc to popula (Supporting detail)
   B. Executive: enforces laws
      1. Pres & VP
      2. Cabinet
   C. Judicial (Supreme Court): judges laws
      1. 9 mems—appntd for life
      2. Appnted by Pres w/consent of Cong
II. Powers given to Congress
   A. _____
   B. _____
   C. _____
      1. _____
      2. _____

---

6. Clarify and expand on your outline notes by taking notes in class on the left-hand side of your notebook. Write down anything stressed by the teacher. Use the same outline form and the same abbreviations.

Here is a brief sample of class notes added to outline notes:

CLASS NOTES	OUTLINE FROM READING
	U.S. Constitution
	I. U.S. Pol. Syst = 3 branches
Ea. Sen elected every 6 yrs. Mem of House elected every 2 yrs.	A. Legislative Congress: makes laws 1. Senate: 100 mems 2 fr ea state 2. House of Reps: 435 mems; acc. to popula.

KNOW FOR TEST
Qual. for Pres
   1.   Native–born U.S. cit.
   2.   35 yrs. old
	B. Executive: enforces laws
	1. Pres. & VP
	2. Cabinet
	C. Judicial (Supreme Court): judges laws
	1. 9 mems, appntd for life
	2. Appntd. by Pres w/consent of Cong

7. *Review* and *edit* your notes as soon after class as you can. [Typing your notes on the computer will help your retention.] Review these notes every day.

8. *Underline* (*or highlight*) important material when studying for a test or an exam.

10 *Four Useful Parts of a Textbook*

The textbook is the core of many courses. Not only is it the primary source of these courses, but it is also a fund of much useful information that many students neglect or overlook.

Here are four things a textbook can tell you:

1. *The way the course is organized* _____

Textbooks invariably give the reader a table of contents. When you receive your book at the beginning of the year, read through the table of contents to learn how the course and the book are organized. As you get into the middle of a course, the table of contents can remind you of the material you have already covered and can tell you what to expect in the future.

2. *The way to find something quickly* _____

Most textbooks have an index in the back, listing all items discussed in the text and giving the pages on which you can find those items easily.

3. *The meanings of terms* _____

Each discipline has its own vocabulary of terms. Textbooks often supply the reader with a glossary, listing those terms and their meanings. The glossary is usually found at the back of the textbook, in front of the index.

4. *Material that words cannot explain* _____

Many textbooks include illustrations, pictures, graphs, charts, maps, or diagrams to explain the written material. In most cases, this material is *not* decorative. It is placed there for a purpose. Use it.

11 *How to Get the Most out of Reading the Textbook*

Reading and learning material from the text is the most basic of study skills. Yet many students have not developed a systematic approach to studying the text. A frequently used unsystematic approach is just to plod through the assigned pages while trying to figure out what the material is all about.

A systematic approach involves *thought* and a conscious effort to attack the material before you begin to read. Instead of turning immediately to the assigned pages, first think to yourself:

> "Why is this material important to what we are studying?"

> "How does this material relate to previous material we have studied?"

> "What are the main points to be considered here?"

A good way to answer these questions (in fact, a good way to begin any assignment in the text) is to turn to the table of contents and see the *ordering* of the material. After the order of the material is clear, you are ready to begin—with book open and pencil in hand [or computer at the ready]—to take notes.

Here are four steps you should take in tackling a textbook reading assignment:

1. Survey

> Glance quickly through the pages immediately preceding the assignment. Pay particular attention to chapter titles and headings in boldface type.

> Read carefully all chapter titles and headings in boldface type in the assigned pages. Glance quickly at the pages following.

> Note any charts, illustrations, or diagrams.

> Note important terms printed in boldface or italics.

2. Question _____

Turn to the end of that section or chapter and carefully note the kinds of questions being asked. Keep the questions clearly in mind when you begin to read.

Make up three or four of your own questions, if the book does not supply them, based on your knowledge of what you think the teacher may consider important or what you think are the most important points. *Write these questions down.*

3. Read _____

Read the text with the above-mentioned questions clearly in mind, underlining or highlighting important material.

Study all charts, illustrations, and diagrams, and know how they fit into the material in the text.

Outline the material using your underlining.

[Typing outlines on your computer will help your retention enormously.]

4. Review (This is the most important step and the one neglected by many students.) _____

Review your notes or underlining *immediately* after completing the reading.

Review your notes or underlining *again* before going to class.

Pay particular attention in class to material you may have missed or misunderstood. Take careful class notes on such material.

Review for tests by briefly glancing over your underlining but *thoroughly* studying your outlining and class notes.

12 Five Problems in Reading the Textbook and How to Solve Them

Most problems in reading and understanding the textbook stem from a lack of an orderly approach, as discussed on pages 58–59. However, even after trying this approach, some students still encounter problems in understanding the material.

Here are five common problems in understanding what you read and suggestions for solving them:

1. "I keep missing the main points."

   Review the headings in boldface type both *before* and *after* reading the assigned pages. Listen closely in class to the points the teacher raises, underline these important points in the book, and write them in your notes.

2. "The text is too hard, too confusing, too complicated."

   It may very well be a difficult text. From the library, get a simplified version of the same material. Read this version, and then go back to the text and see if the material is any clearer. If you have continued problems, see your teacher.

3. "I become lost in a novel or book that has no headings to guide me."

   Most libraries carry plot summaries of (or commentaries on) famous novels and other works of literature. Read one, and then go back to the book and read the assigned pages.

   Libraries also carry novels, short stories, poetry, and plays on tape. Borrow a tape and listen to it as you read along in the book, underlining or highlighting when necessary.

4. "The words are too long and confusing."

   Use the glossary, if there is one. If not, use a dictionary. Write the meanings directly above the confusing words.

5. "I just read too slowly. I'm afraid I'll miss something important."

   Keep a watch or clock handy in front of you as you read. Time yourself. Practice increasing your reading rate every day. (See pages 131–133.)

13 How to Make Abstractions Concrete

Some courses, particularly in the upper grades, deal in difficult abstract ideas. Many of these abstractions, however, can be rendered in concrete form: a chart, diagram, map, or time line. If the material is clarified in class, so much the better. Simply copy in your notebook what the teacher has drawn.

Included below are five examples of how abstract ideas may be rendered in concrete form. The first two examples show that even mathematical abstractions can be given in concrete form. They are certainly not the shortest ways to solve these problems.

Example 1. How many square feet in 4 square yards?

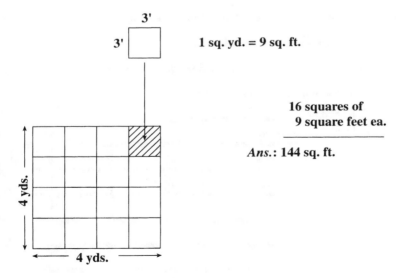

3'

3'

1 sq. yd. = 9 sq. ft.

16 squares of
9 square feet ea.
_____

Ans.: 144 sq. ft.

4 yds.

4 yds.

Example 2. $(a + b)^2 = ?$

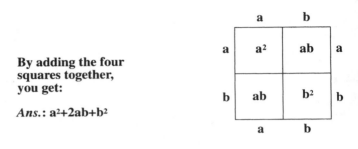

By adding the four
squares together,
you get:

Ans.: $a^2+2ab+b^2$

Example 3. Time line.

In history, time lines can be particularly helpful if the textbook does
not supply one. You can make your own, using material in the text
or from standard reference works such as a world almanac or an
encyclopedia of history.

Here is a time line showing the life spans of U.S. presidents
born since 1865:

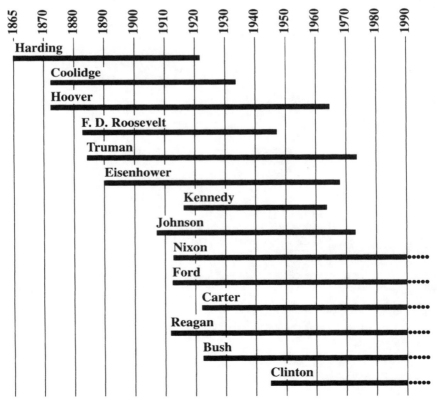

Example 4. Listing.

Often, just a simple list of characters from a book or play can be extremely useful.

Here is an example of the opposing sides in the play *Julius Caesar:*

Conspirators against Caesar	Those Opposing Conspirators	Innocent Bystanders
Marcus Brutus	Mark Antony	Cicero
Cassius	Octavius Caesar	Publius
Casca	Lepidus	Popilius Lena
Trebonius		
Ligarius		
Decius Brutus		
Metellus Cimber		
Cinna		

[This material can be typed on your computer.]

Example 5. Simplified maps.

A freehand map can help clarify and simplify material in history, and even literature, if such material is not included in the book. Here, for example, is a schematic map of the setting for *Huckleberry Finn:*

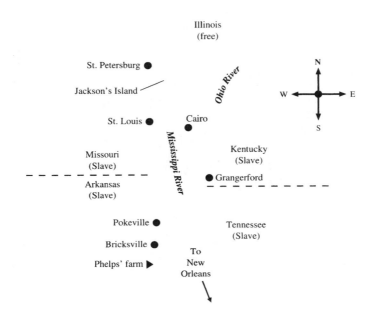

14 *How to Find Answers without Having to Ask Anyone*

If a question comes up as you are studying, there is a good chance you can find the answer by using the materials close at hand. Running around trying to find a teacher or a student who can answer the question can be an enormous waste of time as well as a break in your concentration.

The next time you need an answer quickly, try the following:

Check the index at the back of the book.

Check to see if it is in the glossary, if there is one.

Check the boldface headings in the chapter.

Check to see if it is in your class notes.

Check to see if it is in a supplement in the back of your dictionary.

Check your test and homework papers to see if it appears there.

Check any books on the subject you have taken out of the library.

Check reference books you may have near your study area: almanacs, encyclopedias, and dictionaries (and their supplements).

[Check your computer by bringing up outlines or notes done recently.]

Putting forth some effort to look up an answer is just one more way to strengthen your retention.

UNIT IV

CONCENTRATION

We have met the enemy, and
he is us.

Walt Kelly

65

1   *Five Short Ways to Improve Your Concentration*

We are often our own worst enemy when it comes to providing distractions. Whether from boredom, frustration, or just plain loneliness, many students tend to clutter their lives with distractions that constantly intrude upon their sustained concentration.

Like it or not, sustained concentration is the basic ingredient to successful recall, and good retention is the key to good grades.

Listed below are five short ways to improve your concentration. A word of warning, however: To improve your concentration significantly, *you must follow all five suggestions,* not just one or two.

1. Study in a quiet place, and study in the same place every day. Focus on what you have to study—do *not* daydream.

2. Remove all distractions from your study area. Turn off the stereo or radio, and forget about the TV and telephone while you are studying. [Do not give in to the temptation of playing a game on your computer.]

3. Take a short break after studying for about an hour.

4. Keep a clock or watch handy. Time yourself for each subject, and strive to improve your length of concentration each day.

5. Get help from friends and family in leaving you alone while you are studying. One *major* distraction to concentration is *people.* Another is yourself; so having asked for peace and quiet, *use* your powers of concentration.

NOTE: There is a big difference between daydreaming and mulling over a subject. Daydreaming avoids having to concentrate. Mulling over or pondering a subject is not only useful but virtually necessary for successful concentration.

2 How to Analyze Your Learning Strengths and Weaknesses

The opening pages of this book recognized your uniqueness as an individual. This is not just a statement of faith: Psychologists have studied the ways that people learn, and one psychologist[1] believes that there are as many as seven ways in which we learn. However, for the purposes of this book, we will deal with three areas of perception: visual, auditory, and kinesthetic. Briefly stated, they are sight, hearing, and perception through touch or physical action.

Moreover, psychologists have concluded that for most people one of these areas is stronger than the others and is, in fact, the dominant way of learning. However, people use a combination of all learning modes but tend to rely on one that is strongest in their makeup.

You can test yourself on which area of perception is the dominant one in your makeup by taking the following self-diagnostic test. (Check each item that applies to you.) Then turn to pages 70–71 to discover how you can use your strengths and compensate for your weaknesses.

You are a "sight" learner if you:

☐ Show your emotions by facial expressions.

☐ Follow sports or current events chiefly by reading a magazine or newspaper thoroughly.

☐ Prefer face-to-face meetings or writing notes when you want to express your feelings to someone.

☐ Clam up and sulk when you are angry.

☐ Consider yourself a careful dresser.

☐ Consider note-taking the most important classroom activity.

---

1. Howard Gardner, *Frames of Mind: The Theory of Multiple Intelligences* (New York: Basic Books, 1983).

☐ Would rather watch TV, go to a movie or play, or read a book in your spare time.

☐ Feel most rewarded by the teacher when he or she writes favorable comments on your paper.

You are a "hearing" learner if you:

☐ Show your emotions by talking to someone.

☐ Follow sports or current events chiefly by listening to the radio or watching TV.

☐ Don't mind using the telephone when you want to express your feelings to someone.

☐ Quickly explain to others why you are angry.

☐ Consider yourself a sensible dresser.

☐ Enjoy discussions in class and hearing other points of view.

☐ Prefer listening to the stereo or the radio, attending a concert, playing an instrument, or talking to someone in your spare time.

☐ Feel most rewarded by the teacher when you are praised in class or outside the classroom.

You learn chiefly through physical actions if you:

☐ Show your emotions through body language.

☐ Follow sports or current events by quickly scanning the newspaper or spending a few minutes watching TV.

☐ Like to talk to someone when you are walking or doing some other physical exercise.

☐ Clench your fists or storm off when you are angry.

☐ Consider yourself a comfortable dresser.

(*continued*)

☐ Can't get comfortable in a chair and continually shift position; would rather be somewhere else.

☐ Like to engage in all kinds of physical activity in your spare time.

☐ Feel most rewarded by the teacher who gives you a handshake of congratulations or a friendly pat on the back.

If you have determined from the test above that you learn chiefly by *sight*, here are the units and chapters that should be of help to you:

To capitalize on your strengths:

Outlining the Textbook	Unit III	Chapter	9
Reading the Textbook	Unit III	Chapter	11
"Reading" a Test	Unit VI	Chapter	6
Shifting Speed in Reading	Unit VIII	Chapter	4
Using the School Library	Unit IX	Chapter	1

To compensate for your weaknesses:

Making Abstractions Concrete	Unit III	Chapter	13
Improving Class Concentration	Unit IV	Chapters	4–5

If you have determined from the test above that you learn chiefly by *listening*, here are the units and chapters that should be of help to you:

To capitalize on your strengths:

Improving Class Concentration	Unit IV	Chapters	4–5
Taking Good Class Notes	Unit IV	Chapter	6

To compensate for your weaknesses:

Underlining and Outlining the Textbook	Unit III	Chapters	8–9
Reading the Textbook	Unit III	Chapter	11
Making Abstractions Concrete	Unit III	Chapter	13
"Reading" a Test	Unit VI	Chapter	6
Improving Reading, Writing, Spelling	Unit VIII	Chapters	1–7

If you have determined from the test above that you learn chiefly by *physical action,* here are the units and chapters that should be of help to you:

To capitalize on your strengths:

Making Abstractions Concrete	Unit III	Chapter	13
Getting a Fresh Perspective about			
Your Subjects	Unit VIII	Chapter	1

To compensate for your weaknesses:

Using Time Efficiently	Unit II	Chapter	1
Underlining the Textbook	Unit III	Chapter	8
Reading the Textbook	Unit III	Chapter	11
Improving Class Concentration	Unit IV	Chapters	1–12
Improving Reading Speed	Unit VIII	Chapter	4

7 Five Sure Ways to Improve Your Concentration

Concentration is the result of willpower and requires a great deal of self-discipline. Concentration improves gradually, sometimes slowly, but the important thing to remember is that you can improve this ability by setting specific goals and taking steps for improvement.

The following suggestions are to be used *in addition to* the suggestions on page 67. Here, then, are five steps you can take to improve your concentration:

1. Force yourself to complete everything an assignment calls for, even if it is boring.

2. Imagine that the work is personally important to you and that completing it will bring vast rewards. If you need motivation, set a personal goal—but reward yourself *only* after you have finished a task requiring sustained concentration.

3. Do not daydream. This break in concentration will delay your completing the goal of finishing the assignment.

   NOTE: Thinking through the solution to a problem, organizing ideas in your head, or mulling over the material is *not* daydreaming. On the contrary, this internalized thought process is creative and constructive.

4. Stop working when you are tired. Change your study schedule to make sure you complete the work at a later time—but *be sure to complete it.*

5. Set a specified limit of time for any one subject. For example, set a time limit of thirty minutes for completing your math. Keep a careful watch on the time. If you are able to concentrate only for twenty minutes, increase this time by three or four minutes every day until you are able to reach the goal of concentrating totally for thirty minutes.

4 Six Easy Ways to Improve Your Class Concentration

No skill is more neglected or more difficult to acquire than active listening. We live in an era of constant distractions: TV, radio, the telephone, and people. Added to that, it is probably true that we can listen intently for only very short periods of time without a break in concentration. It is also true that most of us hear what we *want* to hear or *expect* to hear rather than what is actually said.

Good students have developed their techniques for listening closely in the classroom. They know what to listen for and can distinguish between the trivial and the important.

Here are the first steps you should take in improving your class concentration:

1. Sit in the front of the classroom.

2. Sit far away from talkative friends.

3. Sit away from the window.

4. Have your completed homework ready to correct or hand in immediately after taking your seat.

5. Have your notebook open and be ready to take notes. Do not miss the teacher's opening remarks. They are often extremely important.

6. Focus on the teacher and pay close attention to what is being said throughout the class.

5 Ten Sure Ways to Perfect Your Class Concentration

A good way to test your listening ability is to ask yourself what main points the teacher stressed in class the previous day. If you can remember little, chances are you need these ten suggestions to improve your class concentration.

1. Warm yourself up to the subject immediately *before* class by reviewing your notes, your homework, or the underlining you did in the text.

2. Make a game of it. While you are doing your homework, list two or three important items you think your teacher might (or should) bring up in class. During class, check off those items the teacher did, in fact, discuss. If the teacher did not mention one of your items, you have a good reason to raise your hand and ask why the point was omitted.

3. Take notes during class. Follow closely the line of discussion that the teacher takes. Listen for and write down in your class notes the main points made, and also note down any supporting details you have missed in the text.

4. Listen closely for points that a teacher repeats. You are likely to see such points in a question on the next test or quiz.

5. Listen closely when a teacher says, "This is important," or gives other clues to possible test questions. Write such clues in capital letters in your notebook. [Keep the capital letters if you type your notes onto the computer.]

6. Listen for, and copy down, any *new* material the teacher introduces, particularly if the material is not in the text.

7. Listen to other students' questions and remarks, and note especially *the teacher's response to those comments.* If the response is favorable, the student may have hit on something important for you to remember.

8. Take an active part in class discussions, and take careful note of your teacher's response to your questions and remarks.

9. Listen at the end of class when the teacher says, "Well, we did not have time to go into such-and-such today." In the next class, if the teacher does not bring it up first then point out that the topic was not finished previously.

10. Be persistent in developing your listening skills by listening closely to conversations outside the classroom and outside of school.

6

How to Take
Good Class Notes

An important way to improve your concentration in class and to help you on the next test is to take a good set of notes from the remarks the teacher makes. It is a totally mistaken notion that sitting in the classroom and listening intently will provide good retention. In fact, students tested immediately after a class presentation got only 25 percent accuracy on the factual material. As the days pass by, the accuracy drops even lower.

Here are some suggestions for taking a good set of class notes:

- Be ready at the beginning of class to take notes. Have your notebook open and a pencil or pen ready.

- Note down especially the teacher's remarks at the *beginning* and at the *end* of class. These remarks often have to do with important demands of the course such as required reading, quizzes, and tests, or suggestions about how to do the homework.

- Copy down word for word those terms or explanations the teacher has written on the chalkboard.

- Take notes *only* on new material or material that the teacher clarifies. Presumably you have already done the homework, and if you have done it properly you do not need to note down material already in the text or in your notes.

- Listen closely when the teacher says, "That's a good question," "This is important," or other such clues. Jot down such notations in your notebook using such terms as *REMEMBER, IMPORTANT,* or *MEMORIZE.*

- Arrange your notes according to outline form: chapter title at the top of the page, Roman numerals for main ideas, capital letters for supporting details, numbers for subdetails, and small letters for sub-subdetails.

- [Typing your class notes on your computer is a good way to strengthen your retention.]

Here is an example of outline form:

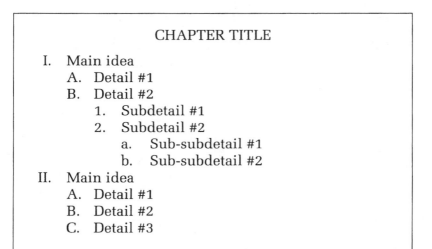

```
                    CHAPTER TITLE

  I.  Main idea
      A.  Detail #1
      B.  Detail #2
          1.  Subdetail #1
          2.  Subdetail #2
              a.   Sub-subdetail #1
              b.   Sub-subdetail #2
 II.  Main idea
      A.  Detail #1
      B.  Detail #2
      C.  Detail #3
```

Here is an example of the way ideas and details should be classified:

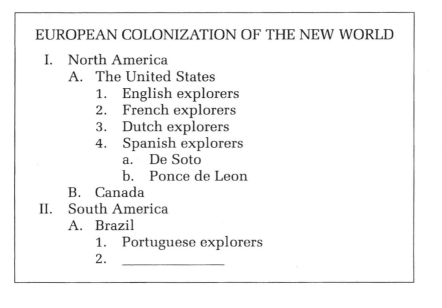

```
    EUROPEAN COLONIZATION OF THE NEW WORLD

  I.  North America
      A.  The United States
          1.  English explorers
          2.  French explorers
          3.  Dutch explorers
          4.  Spanish explorers
              a.   De Soto
              b.   Ponce de Leon
      B.  Canada
 II.  South America
      A.  Brazil
          1.  Portuguese explorers
          2.  _____
```

- Leave five or six lines blank if the teacher starts on a point and becomes sidetracked. Ask politely to return to the point under discussion if the teacher fails to do so.

- Review your class notes as soon as possible after the period has ended.

- Look over your class notes before you go on to any new material or before you begin your homework.

7 *What to Do if You Think the Teacher Is Disorganized*

Students sometimes complain that their failure to concentrate in a course is the teacher's fault. Sometimes this judgment is false, but sometimes it is true.

One complaint that students make is that a teacher is disorganized: that Mrs. X, for example, is difficult to follow in class; that she strays from the subject; that she does not follow what she has assigned in the textbook. If this is truly the case, here are some things you can do to help yourself if you are convinced that the teacher is disorganized:

- Be better organized than the teacher:
  - Do your homework carefully and neatly.
  - Write your tests in a neat and organized manner.
  - Indicate from your remarks in class that you have studied the material thoroughly.

- Do not try to embarrass her by showing off to the rest of the class that you are better organized than she.

- Listen even more intently than usual to such a teacher's remarks. The times that she *does* mention textual material are the times to make note of; such points are more than likely to appear on tests.

- Make certain that she is, in fact, rambling. Perhaps some of what she is talking about appears in a lesson or chapter due later that week. Check the book to make sure.

- Bring her back to the subject by asking her questions on that day's lesson.

- Ask for an appointment to see her. Tell her frankly but politely that you are having difficulty following her remarks in class, and ask for her suggestions.

- Make certain that *you* know the organization of the course by checking the syllabus and by reading the table of contents of the text.

- Be patient with her. She may know that she is disorganized and will appreciate a helping hand.

- Try to put such a teacher in perspective. If she is really as disorganized as you think she is, she probably will not be around the school long. On the other hand, if she has been in teaching for a number of years, you had better think twice: You, not she, may be at fault.

8 *What to Do if You Think the Teacher Is Boring*

Another reason students say they cannot concentrate is that the teacher is boring. The chances are, however, that Mr. X does not *think* he is boring, nor that the subject he teaches is. After all, he has probably devoted a good many years to studying and mastering the subject, and he would probably not have devoted so much time and effort to a field that *he* felt was uninteresting.

If, however, it is your judgment that the teacher is dull, here are some things you can do about it:

- Recognize that, in spite of your judgment of him, the teacher knows a good deal more about the subject than you do.

- Keep your sense of humor. Be alert for those times the teacher is being funny. Enjoy those lighter moments in class.

- Listen closely in class for any new or interesting material.

- Do not just sit passively and think how boring he is. Offer your own insights on the material he is presenting.

- Listen to what other students have to say on the subject. Perhaps they do not find the teacher as boring as you do.

- Do *not* watch the clock. Such a practice will just prolong class time and might offend the teacher.

- Prepare your homework thoroughly. Perhaps one of the reasons you find the teacher boring is that you do not understand what he is presenting in class.

- Make a game of it. As you are doing your homework, list three or more important points you think he might talk about in the next class period. During that class, check off those items he does bring up. Ask him about those points you have listed that he has not mentioned.

9

What to Do if You Think the Teacher Doesn't Like You

It is only natural that you see your situation in class from your own point of view and that the teacher sees it from his or her point of view. Rationalizing your poor concentration in a course by saying that a teacher does not like you is easy to do. In common speech, it is often a cop-out.

The reasoning goes something like this. Mr. X does not like me; therefore I do not like him; therefore I will not work for him; therefore I will do badly in his course, and that will show *him*. The flaw in this logic is obvious: Your failure in his course says more about you than about him. After all, he already has his college degree, and you do not.

There are many reasons for students thinking a teacher may dislike them, but the most common ones are violations of certain expectations that teachers have of their students.

Here are the most common sources of irritation for teachers and what you can do about them:

- Talking in class. Move away from your chatty friends and keep quiet.

- Not doing the work. Most teachers work hard at their craft and resent students who are not willing to put forth effort. Do your work.

- Not saying anything. Maintaining complete silence for days and weeks can be a source of annoyance for some teachers. At least once a day, volunteer some information to let the teacher know you have some interest in what is being taught.

- Sloppy habits. Coming to class late on frequent occasions, forgetting your homework or your books or pencils, and other sloppy behavior is a sure sign to Mr. X that you care little about what he is doing. Although you may not intend it so, he may see such behavior as rudeness and may resent you for it. The solution is easy. Be on time. Do your homework. Don't forget anything.

- Watching the clock. Constantly glancing at your watch or the clock is a certain sign to the teacher that you would rather be elsewhere. Perhaps you *would* rather be elsewhere—just don't show it.

- Personality conflict. Sometimes a teacher and a student just can't seem to get along together. Such a situation is often unavoidable, and you are in the position of having to be in a particular class for the duration of the course. The solution is simple, but it may not be easy for you. Go out of your way to be genuinely courteous to such a teacher, both in and out of the classroom. Make a special effort to do the work. If you put forth a good effort and are polite, the personality conflict may resolve itself.

10 *What to Do if You Think the Teacher Is Unfair*

Another common reason students give for not being able to concentrate is that the teacher is unfair. In some cases, this accusation may be true, but you yourself must be fair-minded enough to recognize that in some cases the fault may be yours.

Here are some common instances where you think the teacher may be unfair, and what you might do about it:

- "She marked something wrong when it should have been right." Keep in mind that teachers know their subjects better than you do. Still, they are prone to making occasional human errors. The solution is easy. Go ask her why she marked the item wrong. If she is fair-minded, she will probably correct the error and regrade the paper.

- "He just didn't understand what I was trying to say." The only way a teacher can judge your work is by what you have written down on the paper. If you have phrased a point badly or have omitted something important, the fault is yours and not the teacher's. However, it is wise to ask for a conference with the teacher and explain what you had in mind. He may not award you extra points, but at least he will understand what you were trying to get at.

- "I think she just enjoys giving out bad grades—especially to me." The grade a teacher gives is just that: a grade. As such, it is only her way of indicating to you what you have (or have not) learned. It is *not* a measure of how good or how nice a person she thinks you are. It is not even a measure of how good a student you are—or even how smart you are. If you get a bad grade, see the teacher at once to find out what you did wrong and how you can avoid such a grade in the future.

- "He keeps taking off too many points on my paper." The probable explanation is that you are making too many mistakes. Go back and carefully review all your test papers and quizzes to see if you can classify the types of mistakes you are making (carelessness, misunderstanding of the material, etc.). When you study for the next test, make sure you know the kinds of mistakes you have been making and try to avoid them. Furthermore, make certain that in the future you read all test directions carefully and do *exactly* what they say.

- "She keeps hassling me by asking me a lot of questions in class. She embarrasses me because most of the time I don't know the answer." Yes, she *is* trying to find out what you know, because that's her job. Why? In all probability, you have a reputation of not doing your work very closely. You can avoid a lot of embarrassment by doing first-rate work. If she is still hassling you after that, go to her and find out why.

11 *What to Do if You Think the Subject Is Boring*

If you are having trouble concentrating because you think the subject is boring, one probable cause is that you have not yet recognized the human element. That is, the subject seems to exist somehow in a vacuum apart from human experience. No matter how dry the subject may seem to be to you, there probably is an interesting human dimension to it.

A second cause of boredom is that you may not have mastered the basic skills or the organization of the subject. Such a lack of skills may make the subject appear to be a jumble of confusing and boring facts.

A third cause of boredom is that you may find the textbook too difficult to read or too dense with factual information.

Here is what you can do in each of these cases:

Humanizing the subject

Try to treat the subject as if it were vital to you personally.

Keep your sense of humor. See if you can find something amusing about the material, particularly with regard to the way humans behave.

Get to know the teacher and find out why the subject is interesting or important to him or her.

Seek help and advice from students who like the subject. Discover why *they* find the material interesting.

Be alert for TV shows (especially public television) that present material in this field.

Read brief biographical sketches of people involved with the subject. Short biographies can be found in the school library.

Mastering the skills

Develop an organized plan of study by:

■ Working on that subject when you are rested.

■ Studying that subject first, at school, so that you can get help from the teacher and other students.

■ Breaking the assignment into half-hour study segments. Do each part at different times, but be sure to complete it.

■ [Drilling yourself on your computer.]

Keep the book with you. Glance at it whenever you have the time.

Read the table of contents to be sure that you understand the organization of the material.

List the skills demanded by the course, and drill yourself on those skills every chance you get.

List and memorize the key questions that the subject asks.

Get help from a fellow student or an adult.

Simplifying a difficult text

Most school libraries carry simplified or popular versions of almost any subject. *HINT:* Versions written for younger children may occasionally be very helpful. Read the simplified version first, and then go back and read your textbook.

Here are some more suggestions:

■ Check your library for tapes, videocassettes, or other audio-visual material pertaining to your subject.

■ Check your library for specialized encyclopedias (for example, in science and technology).

■ [Purchase a software program that will drill you or strengthen your knowledge in your problem subject. Work your way through levels of difficulty in your subject.]

12   *What to Do if You Are "Snowed Under"*

A major block to good concentration is the feeling that you are "snowed under" with work and that, no matter what you do, you cannot possibly cope with the demands of all your subjects. Such a feeling often mistakenly leads to resignation, giving up, or panic.

Here are some suggestions on what you can do about such a situation:

Recognize first that you need help. Seek the help of a friend or advisor.

With your advisor, make a list of your most overwhelming problems. Such a list should go by priority, that is, from the subject demanding the most attention down to the least important one.

Make a plan for attacking each problem in a systematic way:

- Break up longer jobs (term papers, for example) into small, manageable segments, and schedule those segments on a day-by-day basis.

- Do not procrastinate. Work on the segment when you *say* you are going to work on it.

- Try to read more quickly. Scan material that you do not find difficult.

- Go to the teacher and ask if there are any shortcuts you can take that will not hurt your grade.

- Check with your advisor every day, if possible, and talk over the progress you have made.

If these suggestions do not meet your needs, go on to the next unit on pages 94–97 "Managing Stress."

UNIT V

MANAGING STRESS

[Most people] don't know how
to worry without getting upset.
Edith Bunker, character from
All in the Family

1 *Three Short Ways to Ease Excessive Stress*

This discussion of stress is an extension of the previous unit on concentration. Please refer to page 88 to see if your problems are not chiefly stress-related.

If, however, you often feel "stressed out" because of the pressures of school and of your life outside school, try the following:

1. Think over the situation quietly and try to identify the sources of your stress:

   ▪ Is the stress chiefly the result of a particular course? If so, consult your teacher at once, explain your anxiety, and ask for suggestions on ways to reduce your tension.

   ▪ Is your stress primarily the result of pressure at home? If so, talk it over with your parents and ask for their suggestions and cooperation in reducing tension.

2. Bring some physical order or breathing space into your life:

   ▪ Get your academic life in order by organizing your notebook and by cleaning out your files.

   ▪ Cut back on some of your activities if your time is stretched too thin either in school or outside school.

3. Bring some mental order and positive thoughts into your life:

   ▪ Stay away from negative, sarcastic "friends." Instead, try to cultivate those who have a good sense of humor or positive attitude.

   ▪ Ask for suggestions from someone you like and trust.

   ▪ Recognize schoolwork for what it is: a measure of your academic achievement—*not* a measure of your intelligence or your success as a human being.

2

How Bad Is Your Stress?

Stress is as personal and as individualized as you are. Only when stress becomes unmanageable does it get in the way of your progress at school.

Causes. Some kinds of stress we have no control over: extended bad weather, long stretches of darkness in winter, or excessive noise in the environment (living near an airport, for example). Moreover, some stress we either clearly like or we voluntarily permit to ourselves: dieting, competing in sports, or going on a roller coaster. Still other kinds of stress are difficult to manage but are understandable: parents and teachers urging you to do better, for example.

NOTE: Some kinds of self-induced stress are physically harmful. Medical research has produced conclusive evidence that smoking, drinking alcohol, or taking drugs actually *increases* stress.

"Good" Stress. "Good" stress is getting psyched up to meet the challenges of everyday life: competing in sports, performing in a school play, or taking an important test. Such stress is indeed necessary to achieving your individual and scholastic goals.

"Bad" Stress. "Bad" stress is considered any severe anxiety that gets in the way of your academic achievement at school.

Here are some questions you should ask yourself about bad stress:

- Are you so frustrated by the constant hassles of your life that you have trouble concentrating on schoolwork?

- Do you think that your parents or teachers set such high expectations for you that you have little chance of success?

- Do you become very upset or very depressed when you fail a test or paper?

- Do you often try to hide from doing your work—or do you procrastinate frequently?

- Do you panic or draw a blank on tests?

These questions are not intended to identify all (or even most) of the possible conditions of bad stress. They are, however, intended to help you isolate or identify some possible problems.

Specific suggestions for dealing with these and other stress-related problems may be found on pages 94–97.

7

How to Manage Stress at School

This chapter cannot cover all the situations at school that cause undue stress. The techniques recommended here have been used successfully by many students, so remember the theme of this book and put it into practice: You are unique; use whatever works for you.

If you feel stressed out, try to put your schoolwork into perspective. The fact that you are reading this chapter indicates that you are probably a bit overanxious about the consequences of making mistakes or getting bad grades at school. But realize that whatever you have learned thus far in school has not qualified you to be a rocket scientist or a brain surgeon (yet). So whatever poor grades you get will not, thankfully, end in a real-life disaster.

On the other hand, do not put off confronting your problem. Try to do something about it *at once.*

Here are five typical school-related stressful situations and some suggestions on how to handle them:

1. Do you panic on tests?

   ■ Make up some mental jingles and repeat them to yourself before entering the classroom for a test: "If I fail this test, the world won't explode!" "Am I upset now? Not on your life!" Make up your own—the funnier, the better.

   ■ Before you even look at the first question, take three to five deep, lung-filling breaths with your eyes closed. Dangle your arms by your sides to relax the tension. Repeat the deep breathing any time you feel panic returning.

   ■ Read over the test questions before writing anything. Put checkmarks next to the ones you know, *O*s next to the more difficult questions, and *X*s next to the hard questions. Build up your confidence by answering the easier questions first; then go on to the more difficult ones.

2. Are you frustrated by your low grades in one or more of your courses?

   ■ Don't give in to the rationalization, "I'm just not very good at math/science/English/French/whatever." Confront your problem: See your teacher(s) and ask for advice.

   ■ Ask for help from one of your classmates who is good in the subject you are struggling with.

   ■ Try studying at a different time. Your concentration may be out of sync with your body rhythm.

3. Is your social life at school getting in the way of good grades?

   ■ Stay away from those people who put you down, who like to annoy you, or who are sarcastic or negative.

   ■ Be careful of friends who sympathize with you but who gloss over the problem with such advice as, "No problem! Everything will turn out all right. Wait and see." This advice may make you feel better temporarily, but it does nothing to work out your problem. Only *you* can make things turn out all right by taking specific steps to attack your problem.

   ■ Cultivate friends who are cheerful and positive.

4. "What should I do about that horrendous grade on that test/paper? It really upset me."

   ■ Realize that life sometimes plays dirty tricks on us, and the only thing to do is try to learn from our mistakes and forget the bad grade. First, see your teacher to find out where you went wrong and what caused the horrendous grade. Next time, study harder and avoid the same mistakes.

5. "I get anxious when I have to write a paper. Sometimes I get writer's block. I can't even get started."

This subject is treated fully on pages 134–138, "Six Common Problems in Writing and How to Deal with Them."

4 How to Manage Stress outside School

Stress outside school comes from two major sources. The first cause will not surprise you: It's your parents. The second cause will probably surprise you: It's yourself.

Parents. "Why do my parents keep pressuring me to do better?"

- Most parents understandably think that the most lasting and valuable gift they can bestow on their children is a good education. As the postindustrial world becomes more stressful, demanding, and competitive (including, and especially, *their* world), they want you armed with the skills and knowledge that will assure *your* success when *you* get out into the competitive world.

"How can I reassure my parents that I *am* doing my best?"

- First, be sure that you *are* doing your best. Start by trying some techniques of studying suggested in this book.

- Then show your parents specifically the new things you are trying. Point out chapters or units in this book.

- Finally, suggest that, since you *are* trying different ways to improve yourself, it would be better for you if they did not add more pressure to the pressure you are already putting on yourself.

Yourself. You may be a major contributor to your own stress if you do the following:

- Procrastinate a lot

- Daydream frequently

- Put your social life before your academic success

- Blame others for your lack of success

- Plan too many activities outside school

If you are truly interested in changing these barriers to good study habits, get to work now by focusing on one or more of the following units:

- Unit II: Time, pages 17–31
- Unit III: Homework, pages 33–64
- Unit IV: Concentration, pages 65–88
- Unit VII: Carelessness, pages 115–124

5

A Good Exercise for Relaxation

First, lie down on a rug or carpet.

Close your eyes.

Put your hands over your stomach. Take a deep breath.

Let out your breath and feel your hands sink.

Breathe in again. Breathe out. Pause.

Breathe in. Breathe out. Pause.

Now, keeping the rest of your body relaxed, clench your right fist tighter and tighter. (Five seconds) Pause.

Relax.

Now, do the same with your left fist for five seconds. Pause.

Relax.

Now do the same tensing/pause/relaxing technique with various parts of your body:

- Tense your biceps. (Five seconds) Pause. Relax.

- Frown your forehead. (Five seconds) Pause. Relax.

- Clench your teeth. (Five seconds) Pause. Relax.

- Tense your shoulders toward your neck. (Five seconds) Pause. Relax.

- Arch your back. (Five seconds) Pause. Relax.

- Curl your toes and tense your calf muscles. Pause. Relax.

Now, try to keep your mind blank and concentrate only on making each part of your body, one by one, relax: arms, neck, shoulders, face, feet, legs, back. Lie back peacefully (with your mind at rest) for one or two minutes. Then you should be ready to return to work refreshed.

QUIZZES,TESTS, AND EXAMS

There is no failure except in no longer trying.

Elbert Hubbard

DO YOU WANT TO KNOW . . .   **TURN TO PAGE . . .**

1 *Four Easy Ways to Improve Your Test Grades*

Successful test-taking is a skill rarely taught at schools, and students often must learn this skill on their own. Test-taking requires the student to develop three distinct skills: (1) the facility to *recall* material asked for by the test, (2) the ability to *order* the material according to the directions, and (3) the ability to make the best possible use of the *time* allotted you.

Recall requires good memorization, while *ordering* demands an understanding of the facts you have memorized.

Here are four easy ways to meet the demands of a test:

1. Read or write down the material you must recall at least three to six times over a three-day period before the test—not the night before. [Drilling yourself on your computer is excellent for retention.]

2. At the test, read over *all* the questions carefully before writing anything down on paper. Write the answers to all the questions you know well *first,* then go back and do the somewhat hard ones, and then the most difficult ones *last.*

3. Be careful to follow the directions *exactly* as written. Make sure you have answered *all* the questions.

4. Do not waste time struggling over material you find you know absolutely nothing about. Do not try to bluff your way through such a question. Instead, use the time to go back over the material you *do* know and check for careless errors and completeness of answers. *NOTE:* On standardized multiple-choice tests, some teachers feel it is a good idea to guess at most doubtful questions since the penalty for wrong answers is not all that great. *Always* guess on a true-false test since you have an even chance of getting the right answer.

2 *Four Sure-Fire Ways of Memorizing*

Two keys to effective memorization are *repetition* and *pattern.* For example, if you listen once to a song on the radio, the chances are you will be able to remember very few of the words. However, the more often you hear the song, the better chance you have of remembering the words. After you have heard it for the sixth time, there is a good likelihood you can remember most of it.

So, too, with memorization of academic material. You must set up a system that includes constant repetition in a pattern. Such a pattern should be carefully spaced over a duration of time. Educators call this pattern of repetition *reinforcement.*

Here are four techniques of memorizing:

1. Flashcards. This method would be suitable for memorizing vocabulary, simple questions and answers, lists of names and dates, etc. [You can easily adapt this method to your computer.]

   ■ Use flashcards. Purchase a pack of 3" x 5" index cards. Write the questions on one side and the answers on the other to quiz yourself. Examples of flashcards:

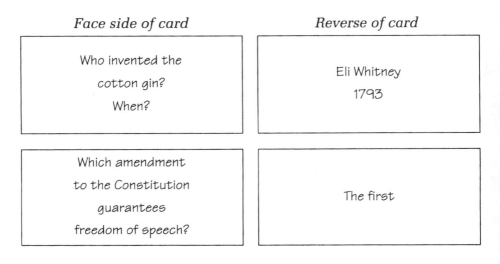

Face side of card	*Reverse of card*
Who invented the cotton gin? When?	Eli Whitney 1793
Which amendment to the Constitution guarantees freedom of speech?	The first

- Place the cards in two stacks as you study: one for the answers you definitely know, another for the answers you do not know. Keep quizzing yourself from the pile you do not know.

- Practice using the flashcards every day, even if you do not have a class in that subject.

2. Listening. Read aloud into a tape recorder the study notes or other material to be memorized. Then listen to the material as many times as you need. Using headphones, you may listen to the tape while you are eating or exercising. A good time to listen is just before you fall asleep.

3. Listing. This technique is suitable for memorizing related facts. [This method may also be adapted to your computer.]

- List one set of facts on the left-hand side of a sheet and the related facts on the right-hand side, as in the example below:

GREEK GODS AND GODDESSES	
LIST A	**LIST B**
Goddess of Beauty	Aphrodite
Father of the Gods	Zeus
Wife of Zeus	Hera
God of the Sea	Poseidon

- Memorize by covering one column with a blank sheet of paper and *writing* down the answers. Check to see which ones you missed, and memorize them by writing out the answer five times.

- Cross-check yourself by covering the other column and then writing out the answers.

[Using the computer, you have the added advantage of easily being able to feed in extra information on any item. For example, for Hera you could type: wife of Zeus/marriage goddess/Greek side, Trojan War. For Aphrodite: beauty goddess/chief supporter, Trojans.

To test yourself, you could call up *beauty* or *marriage* or even try to list which gods and goddesses sided with the Greeks or Trojans.]

4. Mnemonic devices. *Mnemonics* is just a word for an easy way to remember things. Teachers often supply such shortcuts in class. When they do, copy them and use them. Here are a few examples of these memory methods:

   - The names of the metrical feet in poetry: I-T-A-D-S, standing for iambic, trochaic, anapestic, dactylic, and spondaic.

   - The colors of the spectrum: ROY G. BIV, standing for red, orange, yellow, green, blue, indigo, violet.

   - Spelling words correctly offers numerous examples:
     - There is always "a rat" in "sep*arat*e."
     - The "princi*pal*" is a *pal.*
     - Breaking up words: Connect-I-Cut = Connecticut

   - Make up your own sentence for items to be memorized. If you had to memorize the eight parts of speech (Noun, Pronoun, Adjective, Verb, Adverb, Preposition, Conjunction, Interjection), you might make up a sentence that reads: No Pigs Are Valiant After People Cause Injuries.

In short, use any mnemonic device that you find useful, but *keep it simple.* The more complicated the system, the less chance you have of memorizing successfully.

7 The Best Ways to Use Your Notes for Tests

You should have two sets of notes: those taken in class and the outlining or underlining you have done from the text. The length and the accuracy of these notes determine just how effectively you can study from them.

Class notes are very important since they frequently clarify and explain material *not* included in the text. Moreover, class notes often give a strong indication of what the teacher thinks is important and what might be on the test.

Here are ways you can best use the kinds of notes you have:

Good set of outlining/good set of class notes. For the most part, you are free of the text and should use the book *only* for reference or to check the accuracy of factual material.

- Using your class notes as a guide to what is important, underline in red or highlight all important material.

- Note particularly items that you find confusing or difficult to memorize.

- Then go back and carefully read all your underlining, paying particular attention to trouble spots. (You may have to check the text for these areas.)

- Finally, quiz yourself by choosing a particular topic to see if you can reproduce your notes exactly. [You may want to use a computer to test yourself.]

- After the test, check off those sections in your notes that appeared on the test.

- When your test is handed back, edit and correct your notes for errors and inaccuracies.

Good set of class notes/good underlining. In this case, the class notes serve as your principal guide on what to study.

- Read your class notes and try to predict what might be asked on the test.

- With the class notes as a guide, read *only* those sections of the text that appear in your class notes.

- Read through all your underlining.

- Repeat the second step.

- Quiz yourself by taking a topic at random, and see if you can write it completely and accurately *in outline form.* [You may want to use your computer to quiz yourself.]

Poor set of class notes/good outlining or underlining. Before you do anything else, sit down and make a list of *all* the topics you can remember that were discussed before the test. Try to recall also about how much of the class period was spent on each topic. Perhaps you should check with a fellow classmate. Then follow one of the two procedures above as if you had a good set of class notes.

Poor set of class notes/poor underlining or outlining. You are in a desperate situation, but you might be able to pull yourself out of it with time and hard work.

- List all the topics you recall discussed in class, particularly ones that took most of the class period. Check with a classmate.

- Go to the text and read carefully *(at least three times)* all of the topics that you have listed. Make time to write a brief outline of the material. [Use your computer—it's faster.]

- Quiz yourself on the material by answering the questions at the end of the chapter or section. [Use your computer to test yourself.]

- Take out your old tests and quizzes to see if you can predict the kinds of questions that will be on the test.

- When you get into the test, jot down *immediately* in the margins any material relevant to the questions. Then go back and answer more fully, if needed.

- Leave those questions blank that you cannot recall at all. Instead, try to get as many points as you can by answering accurately and fully the questions you do know.

- When you get the corrected test back, put in your notebook the full and correct answers to anything you missed.

4 *How to Predict What Might Be on a Test*

There is no way you can be 100 percent certain what questions might be asked on a test. However, if you are alert, you might be able to catch indications of the types of questions that could be asked.

The surest indicator is the teacher, and most successful test-takers are careful teacher-watchers. The material often dictates the kinds of questions that may be asked. For example, many tests and quizzes in beginning language courses are likely to be on vocabulary, grammar, verb tenses, etc. Even language teachers sometimes tip their hand, so be alert in class.

Here are some ways to tell what might be asked on a test or quiz:

1. Listen closely any time a teacher says, "This is important," "You must know this," or other such clues. Of course, the absolute giveaway is when the teacher says, "This will be on the test." Mark this down in your class notes. Listen carefully to the *approach* Mr. X takes in discussing the material.

   - Does he talk chiefly about factual data, or in generalities such as "motivation," "causes," and so forth?

   - Does he place important emphasis on student writing? If so, be on the alert for essay questions.

   - Does he stick closely to the text, or does he stress supplementary material such as historical background?

   - Does he use the chalkboard a lot? If so, *copy* everything he writes.

   - Does he give handouts in class? If so, put them in a prominent place in your notebook and study them.

   - How has he responded to other students' questions? Take note if he has answered positively with, "That's a good question" or some other clue.

2. Look back over the corrections he has made on your past quizzes and tests.

- See if you can discover a pattern to the kinds of questions he asks: all factual, all essay, or part factual and part essay?

- See if you can discover a pattern to the *remarks* he has made on your test papers.

- See if you can discover where he places the most emphasis: on defining terms, on people, on institutions, on reasons, on effects, etc.

If you can keep in mind each teacher's points of emphasis, you can often predict the kinds of questions that may be asked. You will probably do better on your tests if you gear your studying to such points of emphasis.

5 How to Make the Best Use of Test Time

Taking a test usually involves your having to finish in a stipulated period of time, in many cases a class period. Such a pressure situation sometimes causes a student to become frustrated or to panic.

You can function well under the pressure of time with a little practice and a rational approach to testing. The surest way to avoid panicking is to know the material well and to bring to the test a feeling of mastery and confidence. However, even some students who know the material well have not mastered the method of working under the pressure of time. (If you have serious anxiety in taking tests, see pages 89–98.)

Here are some ways you can best use the time allotted in a test:

- Be sure to have a watch if there is no clock in the classroom.

- Read over the test thoroughly before writing anything. If the relative importance of the questions is indicated, note those items that are more heavily weighted.

- Divide your time according to the weighting of the material and how much you know. (If you know nothing on one question, it is probably wise to leave it blank and spend the time writing what you *do* know or have at least some knowledge of.)

- In the margins, make brief notations of material you know you must include before you forget it. Most teachers permit such notations right on the test sheet.

- Decide in what order you plan to answer the questions. Write the answers first to the questions you know well, then to the ones you know less well, and then last, to the difficult ones.

    Teachers generally do not care in what order you take a test. They are chiefly interested in what you know, not in what order you answer the questions. (Furthermore, some teachers mark their papers by sections rather than in numerical order. That is, they will grade, say, all Part II essay questions of a class at one time.) Deciding on the time and the order to take the test should require only a few moments.

- As you take the test, try to keep as closely as you can to the schedule of time you have set for yourself. If you spend more time on one question than you had planned, you must then take away some time from another question, usually one on which you are weak.

- Try to leave enough time at the end of the test to check for accuracy and completeness—usually about five minutes.

6

How to "Read" a Test

"Reading" a test is another skill that must be mastered before you can expect good grades. There are really two parts in reading a test: preliminary scanning of the entire test before you begin writing, and understanding *exactly* what the directions call for.

The preliminary scanning of the questions is primarily to decide the amount of time you plan to spend on each question and the order in which you plan to write the answers.

Understanding the directions may at first seem simple, but most teachers have already decided in the questions the kinds of answers they are looking for. It is up to you to determine as precisely as possible how to form your answers.

Here are some suggestions about the ways to read a test properly:

- Spend a few moments analyzing each question. Ask yourself, "What is the major point the teacher had in mind in making up this test?"

- Jot down brief notes of the major point the question is asking for and all the supporting evidence you can think of that relates to that point.

- Try to think of past tests where similar questions were asked. Can you apply the same technique you used before?

- Make a determined effort to write *exactly* what the question asks and no more. Putting down *more* than is asked for is probably a waste of time and will usually not earn you a better grade.

- Know the terminology for essay questions and follow the instructions exactly as written.

Here are some of the more frequently used terms in essay questions:

Compare. Point out similarities and perhaps a difference or two between the things being compared.

Contrast. Point out the differences and perhaps one or two similarities between the items being contrasted.

Define. Usually, give the book definition of a term. If not, give a short meaning of the term, or a synonym.

Describe. Write the physical characteristics clearly or relate the events as you would in a story.

Diagram. Draw a picture of what is asked and label where necessary.

Discuss. Analyze a point carefully and in detail. Give all of the pertinent supporting evidence you can think of.

Evaluate. Being as objective as you can, give your judgment of a point. Bring in both sides of a question and indicate which one you prefer.

Explain. Make a point clearly by giving reasons, particularly regarding causes, motivation, etc.

Illustrate. Usually means to give specific examples of why something is true. Sometimes means to draw a diagram or picture.

List. Just that. Make a list. No other written explanation is necessary or required.

Prove. Often used in mathematical proofs. The same technique applies. Show that something is true by giving specific examples in a logical pattern.

Relate. Show how different things all have something in common.

State. Write the key points in a question. (Often this is followed by a statement such as, "Give reasons for your answer.")

Summarize. Briefly state the main points of a chapter, the plot of novel or short story, or the events in a narrative. Do *not* go into excessive detail.

Trace. Usually followed by " . . . the development." Show the progress from one historical time to another.

7

How to Eliminate Cramming for Exams

Last-minute cramming for exams may bring you some feeling of confidence about your grasp of a subject, but it is very doubtful that it does much good in actually learning or reviewing the material.

Cramming is often the result of panic started by fellow students, and this feeling of anxiety can spread quickly and affect your ability to work the way you should. You can sometimes avoid such panic simply by walking away and trying to get an objective view of the situation. Try to develop a calm, logical approach to studying for exams.

If you think it necessary to study with another student, choose someone who has a calm and orderly approach to reviewing for exams. Avoid those students who say (even as a joke), "I am going to fail this exam."

Here are five steps you should take to eliminate cramming for exams:

1. Use a calendar to write down the exam schedule *at least a week* before studying for the first exam. Such a schedule should capitalize on your strengths and compensate for your weaknesses:

   - Schedule the most time for subjects you are doing poorly in and must pass.

   - Schedule the least amount of time for subjects you are doing well in and for which you can afford a shaky exam grade.

   - Schedule subjects in one-hour study segments. After each hour, take a short break. After four hours of studying, take a long break including exercise.

   - Schedule difficult subjects during those times of the day when you feel freshest.

   - Schedule your good subjects every other day. Schedule your weak subjects every day, and twice the day before the exam.

2. Follow the schedule exactly as you have written it. Do not panic and start studying a subject just because someone says, "So-and-so told me that such-and-such is sure to be on the exam!" Keep cool.

3. Develop an order of attack for each subject by writing down ahead of time exactly what you plan to study and in what order. Here is one such order:

   - Go through and review all tests and quizzes, noting those on which you did not do particularly well. Reread those sections of the text immediately.

   - Underline the main points of the test questions on which you did well. Keep them for your final-night's review.

   - Reread and underline your class notes. Keep them for a final review the last night before an exam.

   - Go through the table of contents of the text, checking off in pencil the material you do not remember well. Read that material, underlining the important points.

   - [Use your computer to quiz yourself on material that must be memorized.]

   - Use your last hours of study for a short review of the underlining on your tests, your class notes, and the text.

4. Go to bed early. Fatigue destroys concentration.

5. When you take the exam, use the same technique as was recommended for taking a test (see pages 109–110).

UNIT VII
CARELESSNESS

Close only counts in horse-
shoes and hand grenades.
Modern-day aphorism

115

1 *Ten Short Ways to Cure Carelessness*

Sloppy work habits are not easy to cure quickly, for they are often ingrained into our living pattern. It takes a conscious effort to overcome these careless patterns, and a recognition that such an effort may take time.

Generally, careless work habits in students take two forms: in the sloppy ways they conduct their affairs at school, and in the careless mistakes they sometimes make over and over again.

Here are some steps you can take to overcome carelessness:

- Take a few minutes at the beginning of the school day to plan out what you are going to do that day.
- Think ahead to your classes. Remember to bring to class *everything* you need: books, notebook, calculator, pencil or pen, etc.
- Be prompt to class. Have your book or notebook open at the beginning of each class. Settle in to the subject immediately.
- Make sure your desk and notebook are well organized so that you can find anything you need immediately.
- Always leave a few moments at the end of a test or quiz to check your work.
- Proofread all written work before you hand it in. [Use a spell-check or grammar-check.]
- Keep a list of your most frequent careless errors—*by subject*—in the front section of your notebook. Keep each list in front of you when you are doing your homework or writing a paper. [Keep such a list prominently displayed on your computer.]
- Do *not* use separate notebooks for each subject. The best way to keep your notes is in one three-ring binder.
- Keep all your corrected papers *in the same place.* Never fold the papers and stuff them into your textbook, or leave them unfiled in the notebook.
- Keep an orderly locker at school. Put all books and notebooks in the same place every day.

2 *Five Common Careless Mistakes and How to Correct Them*

Carelessness is a continuing nuisance to teachers and a constant source of frustration to students. Rightly or wrongly, if a paper is messy a teacher will often get the impression that a student does not care and will sometimes mark accordingly.

Moreover, neat papers—especially those done [on the computer] with proper margins and double-spacing—tend to receive higher grades than do sloppy papers with the same quality of work.

This may seem unfair, but a meticulous paper often suggests to the teacher that the student *cares* about the work and *respects* the teacher enough to turn in a neat assignment.

In science and math, careless errors appear most often as miscalculations. In written work and on essays, they take the form of misspellings and sloppy punctuation. Five causes of student carelessness are:

1. A feeling that attention to detail is unimportant either to the student or to the teacher.

2. Mismanaging time so that when a paper is due, there is no time to proofread, edit, or check for accuracy.

3. Jumping ahead too quickly in a math problem or in writing a sentence or paragraph.

4. Forgetting the questions asked and going off on a tangent.

5. A temporary lapse in memory or concentration.

The results of carelessness can be costly to you personally. Bad grades may be the only penalty now, but later in life submitting a sloppily punctuated application to a college or a poorly spelled resume to a potential employer may very well dash hopes you have for yourself.

The following three pages offer some suggested solutions to the five problems outlined above.

Attention to detail

- Convince yourself that attention to detail is important to you personally.

- Set up your handwritten papers in an orderly fashion, using the margins of the paper as a guide, and using the lines for your work.

- [Use proper margins, standard font, and double-spacing for all typed papers. (See page 143 for Standard Manuscript Format.)]

- Leave plenty of white space on your paper in case you want to add something or correct something later. For the first draft of a paper, for instance, write on every other line or double-space typed papers. On math papers and tests, do not cram your numbers together. Write large, and leave plenty of blank space for figuring calculations.

- Keep a list of your most common careless errors in the same place in your notebook. Check the list every time you do your homework. [Program your computer spell-check for words you frequently misspell. Or use the *Find* command to check homonyms and reversals: *from/form* and *their/there,* for example.]

- Proofread all written work before handing it in. If you are weak in spelling and punctuation, have someone competent proofread for you and point out your mistakes, but correct them yourself. [Use the grammar-check on your computer, if your school permits.]

Mismanagement of time

- Set up a study schedule for long projects such as term papers, and keep to that schedule. Be sure to leave enough time at the completion of the paper to check for accuracy of facts, punctuation, grammar, and spelling.

- Use such marginal notations as question marks on a test to remind you to check a particular point before you hand in your paper.

- Allow yourself enough time at the end of a test to check your marginal notations and the accuracy and completeness of your answers.

- Do not put off trying to manage your time more usefully. If you need a new schedule of study, draw one up *now.* You will make life easier for yourself and will be able to cut down on careless errors at the same time. (See pages 26–29 for ways to set up a monthly calendar and weekly schedule.)

Jumping ahead too quickly

- Read the directions of a test *twice,* once for meaning and once to underline the key words and phrases of the question.

- Jot down brief notes of *exactly* what you plan to write.

- Jot down in the margin new ideas that come to you as you are writing, but do *not* include them in the middle of the material you are discussing. Include new ideas at the end of the material you are discussing *only* if you think they are essential to the question being asked.

- In math and science, use your common sense when you look at your answer. If, for example, the problem involves filling a car's tank with gas, and your answer is $217.80, something has to be wrong. Go back and check your decimal points and calculations.

Going off on a tangent

- Read the directions of a test *twice,* once for meaning and once to underline the key words and phrases.

- Jot down brief notes of what you plan to write, and *stick to them.* Make sure your notes conform exactly to what the question asks.

- Set a time limit for each question, and *stick to it.*

- Leave enough time at the end of the test to *reread the directions* and your answers. Immediately cross out material that does not apply to the question.

Lapse in memory or concentration

- You may be working too quickly and feel the pressure of time too keenly. Stop working. Take a deep breath. Pause for a few moments.

- Put a question mark in the margin if you cannot think of an answer you *know* you know. Leave enough blank space to finish the answer later. Then go on and do a question you know well. This might restore your confidence, and the answer you forgot might pop back into your mind.

- If the answer never does come to mind, write it off to experience. If it is something like mixing up the names of the characters in a book or forgetting a name, you probably will not lose many points if your answer to the rest of the question is good enough.

- Make a point of doing your homework carefully before a test. Your memory lapse may be the result of not being familiar enough with the material.

- Be as neat as you can under the pressure of time. A cluttered paper tends to befuddle the thinking process and may lead to such a lapse.

7 How to Stop Making the Same Mistakes Over and Over Again

Making the same mistakes over and over again is a sure sign of careless thinking. It is also costly for your grade: Instead of being penalized just once, say for five points, you could keep accumulating the same five-point penalty by making the same mistake again and again until it has a telling effect on your course average.

Here are some suggestions for eliminating those errors that keep repeating themselves:

Recognize that whatever you have tried to do to correct the mistake is not working. Try one of the following:

- Use a mnemonic device (see page 104). Simple example: If you cannot remember $9 \times 8 = 72$, try memorizing the first consonants: Nine Eights = Seventy-Two (N-E-S-T).

- Try to put the mistake you are making in a new context, or rephrase it. Same example: "Ninety-eight cents is now worth seventy-two cents," or "My number on Careless Street is 98-72."

- Try drawing a picture of it. Try writing it larger:

$$9 \times 8 = 72$$

Do it in reverse order: $72 = 8 \times 9$.

- Keep a brief list of your most common mistakes handy as you do your work. Cross off those you have mastered. [This can be done easily on your computer.]

   Make notations at the top of your test papers of the three most common careless mistakes you make in that subject. Examples: *Check spelling, Check periods.* In math: *Check positive and negative signs.* Glance at these notations (especially before a test) to make certain you do not make the same mistakes again. [Program the spell-check on your computer to include words you frequently misspell.]

4 *How to Remember Where You Put Things*

It is easy for most people to remember where they have put things that are important to them: their wallets, their cars, or their jewelry. Things that are valuable to people often get a high degree of attention as to where they are placed.

Many students do not place a high degree of value on where they put their school things, either because they do not care much or because they think there are just too many books, papers, and things for them to keep track of efficiently.

Here are some suggestions to prevent you from carelessly misplacing the things you need at school:

- Make a conscious effort not to accumulate junk. Throw away *everything* in your locker you no longer need.

- Always put the same things in the same places.

- Organize the spaces you need in an orderly manner (see pages 40–41).

- Keep your personal effects separated from your academic paraphernalia.

- Think in terms of parts, not the whole. Don't think about how many books you have to carry. Instead, think only about such-and-such a subject: For any subject, you need only the textbook, your notebook, and something to write with.

- Think in terms of parts of the day, not the whole. If your first two periods are math and Latin, for example, you need only two textbooks, your notebook, pencils, and possibly a calculator.

- Check your bookbag or totebag before class to make sure you have everything you need.

- Keep all textbooks in the same place and in the same order.

- Try to get a seat in the homeroom next to someone who is organized. Disorganized students next to you have a way of borrowing books they have forgotten to bring.

- Keep your homework assignments handy and in the same place when you pack up your books to take home.

- Remind yourself of Henry David Thoreau's advice over a hundred years ago: "Simplify! Simplify! Simplify!"

UNIT VIII

Everybody is ignorant, only in different subjects.

Will Rogers

ACADEMIC SUBJECTS

1 *Three Ways to Get a Fresh Perspective about Your Subjects*

No one can *command* you to become interested in your subjects if you find them tedious and difficult. However, the most useless thing you can do if you find your schoolwork dreary is just to complain about the work or gripe about the teachers and the school.

What you *can* do is take a personal interest in yourself and try to *do* something about the situation. Here are three ways to get a fresh perspective about your subjects:

1. Realize that whatever subject you are taking has existed for a long time *apart* from your school.

2. Try to see that every subject has a distinctly human element.

   ▪ The most human element representing the subject is the teacher. Try to come to know the teacher personally and ask *why* he or she was attracted to a particular subject.

   ▪ Read biographical accounts (there are some brief ones) about the lives of the people who were active in the subject you are studying. Like you, they had difficulties and faced the same kinds of problems: family, work, money, frustration, etc.

   ▪ Talk to friends of your parents. Find out what they do and how they became interested in the subject.

   ▪ Talk to your friends at school who like the subject. Perhaps they can advise you on how to increase your interest and effort.

3. Make a conscious effort to relate what you have learned in school to your everyday life:

   ▪ Use math for doing carpentry.

   ▪ Compare fictional characters you have read about to people you know.

   ▪ Relate what you have learned in American history to the places you have visited.

2

How to "Warm Up" to a Subject

Many students begin to study a subject cold. They arrive at class without prior preparation—their minds still on last night's TV program, on yesterday's game, or on the countless distractions that everyday life provides.

Warming up to a subject is just as important to the student as to the athlete who must warm up before a game or a practice. Not only does it limber the muscles, it provides one with a positive frame of mind to pursue the activity. So, too, the student should practice a warm-up.

Here are some guidelines to use to warm up to a subject:

- Put other distractions aside before beginning to study your homework.

- Take a few minutes before starting your homework to think back to that day's class. Try to recall specific points that were raised. Review your class notes.

- Devise a methodical plan for how you are going to attack the homework (see pages 38–39).

- Take a few minutes before class to plan out your schedule of work for the day. Are there any long-term projects that need your attention?

- Check over your notes before entering the classroom.

- Chat with another student about the main points of the previous night's homework.

- Enter the classroom ready to work. Have all the books you need, as well as pencils, notebook, etc.

- Zero in immediately on the teacher's opening remarks. Can you recall any topic that the teacher should have discussed the day before?

7
Seven Ways to Improve Your Spelling

There is no one or sure method of improving spelling. The arrangement of letters in English words frustrates many people, and the best way to approach spelling is to be determined to do it right by whatever methods work for *you.*

The methods suggested below, then, are not to be used in any order. Use the two or three or more methods that best suit you.

1. Here is a list of commonly misspelled, nuisance words. Underline the ones you consistently misspell, copy them, and keep them in a prominent place in your notebook. [Enter them on your computer and bring them up on the screen before you write a paper to hand in.]

ACCEPT this gift/ everyone EXCEPT me
A LOT (never *alot*)
ALL READY to leave/he had ALREADY gone
ALL RIGHT (never *alright*)
ARE you well?/come to OUR house
BEGINNING of the *inning*
BELIEVE it or not
DOCTOR (not-ER)
DOES he or DOESN'T he like candy? (not *dose*)
ESCAPE (not *excape*)
FEBRUARY
FRIEND
GRAMMAR (not -ER)
HEAR with your *ear*/HERE is not *there*
HOLE in one's head/the WHOLE thing
IT'S (it is) raining/the team and ITS coach
KNOW the answers/NO way out
LOSE the game/LOOSE as a goose
NEW shoes/she KNEW the answer
OF mice and men/OFF to the races
OF the school/could HAVE (not *of*) gone
PAST is not present/he PASSED the gravy
PIECE of pie/PEACE in our time

RECEIVE a letter
SEPARATE (sep-a-rate)
SUPPOSED TO (with the *D*)
THEN what happened?/bigger THAN I am
THERE he is/THEY'RE (they are) smart/THEIR books
THREW a pitch/THROUGH the tunnel/THROW a ball
TO go TO bed/TOO hard for me/TWO dollars
TUESDAY
USED TO (with the *D*)
WEAR warm clothes/WHERE are you?
WEATHER forecasting/I don't know WHETHER to go
WEDNESDAY
WE'RE (we are) leaving/we WERE going
WHICH one? (not *wich* or *witch*)
WHOSE book is this?/WHO'S (who is) the captain?
WOMAN (only one)/WOMEN (more than one)
WON a prize/ONE dollar
WRITE a letter/my RIGHT hand
WRITING a letter/a WRITTEN report
YOUR books/YOU'RE (you are) welcome

2. Memorize the spelling rules of words that give you the most trouble: *I before E except after C,* for example. The problem here, as with most spelling rules, is that there are exceptions: *either, leisure, neither, seize, weird*—illustrated mnemonically by *neither leisured foreigner seizes the weird heights.* Most grammar books carry such rules and their exceptions.

3. Use mnemonic (memory) devices:

   - A *PIE*ce of *PIE*

   - There's A RAT in sep*ARAT*e.

   - The princi*PAL* is a PAL.

   - Station*E*ry is for l*E*tt*E*rs.

   - *HERE* and t*HERE* and everyw*HERE*

   - Have seconds on de*SS*ert.

   - Break up words: disc-rim-in-ate, re-commend-ation

   - Mary made a sum*MARY.*

   - And so on. Write down your own list and keep it in a prominent place in your notebook.

4. Practice writing out (five or more times) words you frequently misspell. [Program your computer for these words.]

5. Keep an alphabetical listing of your own frequently misspelled words in your notebook and glance at it frequently.

6. Use a dictionary often. Note carefully how the word is pronounced and divided, and stress the syllable you misspell: e.g., mis-chie-*VOUS* (three syllables only).

7. Ask a good speller to proofread your written work for mistakes, but *correct the errors yourself.* [Some people, by nature, just seem to be poor spellers. Learn to type on a computer and use the spell-check if you are such a person.]

4

How to Shift Speed in Reading

Reading everything assigned at school at the same speed is inefficient and probably wastes a lot of your time and energy. It is something like running a car's engine in high gear (or low) at all times regardless of traffic conditions.

One way to begin shifting speed in reading is to recognize the kind of material suitable to each speed:

> *Fast reading:* newspapers, magazines, and periodicals; popular novels and short stories; skimming for content.

> *Medium speed:* popular books on difficult subjects; novels assigned in class, and literature.

> *Slow speed:* scientific articles; some textbooks; poetry.

Here is a way to test yourself on your speed, especially in the medium and slow categories. With a watch or clock in front of you, read ten pages of the material. Do not look at the watch as you read. After you have finished, calculate the number of pages per minute you have read. Try to increase your rate every day while trying to maintain maximum comprehension. You can informally test your comprehension of the material in two ways:

1. Go back and closely reread the ten pages and see how much of the important material you missed.

2. Listen closely in class for the points the teacher discusses, noting the points you caught and the ones you missed.

Analyze the kinds of problems you are having and devise a plan for attacking them:

■ **Reading each word.**   Many   students   have the   problem   of   reading   every   word printed   on   the   page   instead   of   reading by   groups   of   words   or   phrases.

First, practice reading by groups of two or three words, thus: *Many students*   *have the problem of reading every word*   *printed on the page instead of reading*   *by groups of words*   *or phrases.* Then, as you get better, you can develop your skill by reading larger groups of words, thus:
Many students have the problem   *of reading every word printed on the page*   *instead of reading by groups of words and phrases.*

- **Subvocalization.** Subvocalization is a habit left over from grade school when you were first taught to read aloud. It is sounding out words in your head, often moving your lips when you do so. There is nothing *wrong* with subvocalizing except that it tends to slow down your reading rate. Reading by groups of words (described above) is one way to stop subvocalizing.

- **Regression.** Regression is reading to the middle of a sentence or paragraph, forgetting what came before, and going back and rereading what you think you missed. Students sometimes regress in their reading when they are afraid of missing something important or when their minds are not focused closely on the main ideas in the lesson.

Here are several ways to improve your reading.

First, try to train your eye not to reread passages. Keep reading. Sometimes the point is clarified or repeated later in the paragraph, or summarized at the end of the chapter.

Second, focus on the topic sentence of each paragraph, usually the first sentence. This sentence announces the main idea of the paragraph and should be underlined and kept in mind as you read.

Third, do not be overly concerned about missing something important. There is a good chance that this important point will be discussed and clarified in class.

Fourth, be certain to scan the headings in large type in the text. These headings will give you clues as to those things that are important.

Fifth, look for these word clues that the author gives in discussing the material:

Speed-up words.   These words signal that there is going to be more of the same:

also	likewise	and
more	again	more than that
moreover	furthermore	in addition

Slow-down words.   These words signal that you should slow down because a change in ideas is about to occur:

but	nevertheless	rather
although	despite	however
yet	in spite of	

Here-it-comes words.   These words signal that a summary or conclusion is about to be stated:

| so | therefore | accordingly |
| thus | consequently | in summary |

Last, exercise good judgment. If you *know* that the passage is important and you have difficulty understanding it, go back and reread the entire passage.

5 Six Common Problems in Writing and How to Deal with Them

"Easy writing makes damned hard reading," observed Lord Byron. Developing the techniques for writing well may take time, so if you have problems expressing yourself clearly, you might want to deal with only one or two problems at a time.

Here are six common problems in writing and what you can do about them:

1. *Writing block*

   If you have problems setting anything down on paper, here are some suggestions:

   - You may be too anxious. Take a 15-to-20 minute break and think through your topic in a quiet setting.

   - Now jot your thoughts down in random order. Do not be concerned about sloppiness or misspellings at this stage. [The computer is excellent for this process.]

   - Then begin to organize your random jottings by writing an outline (see pages 137–138) *even if it is not required.*

   If you are in the middle of a paper and are suddenly blocked, try the following:

   - Take a short break. Do your work in another subject. Then return to your paper.

   - Try writing the final paragraph. This might give you the sense of direction you need.

   - Look at your outline and see if there is a section you can skip ahead to.

2. *Writing poor introductions and conclusions*

   These two important paragraphs demand special attention.

   - An introductory paragraph should always explain clearly the main idea of the paper and suggest its design and organization.

■ A concluding paragraph should be a summary of the main idea expressed in the opening paragraph. It also often calls for some judgment or evaluation of the material discussed.

If you have trouble writing introductory and concluding paragraphs, try writing the introduction *last.* If you have trouble writing the concluding paragraphs, try writing them *first.* Of course, when you have finished your paper, you should go back and revise what you have written.

3. *Weak opening sentences*

In answering essay questions on tests and quizzes, students sometimes have a way of jumping into the middle of the discussion without having first introduced the idea. The rule is: Always repeat part of the question in the opening sentence of your answer, thus:

Question: Discuss three major causes of the Civil War.

Opening sentence: Three major causes of the Civil War were . . .

In longer essays, the main idea and all essential information should be introduced in the first paragraph.

Sample topic: Discuss the mixture of sadness and humor in *Winnie the Pooh,* by A. A. Milne.

Sample introduction (Main idea in topic sentence. Sentences following give essential information: title, author, main characters.):

Life is a mixture of sadness and humor. This idea was illustrated in the characters in *Winnie the Pooh,* by A. A. Milne. This book concerns the adventures of Christopher Robin, his friends Pooh, Piglet, Eeyore, and others who live in a forest near . . .

4. *Straying from the topic*

If you keep the main idea of the paper clearly in mind, you can avoid getting off the subject (sadness and humor, for example) simply by repeating a word or phrase from your subject in the topic sentence of each paragraph. Here are some examples of topic sentences:

■ "The funniest example of sadness was the time when. . . . "

- "However, the only time Christopher Robin was sad was. . . . "

- "Piglet's most humorous scene was. . . . "

5. *Inappropriate style*

Students sometimes want to impress the teacher by using fancy words or phrases that are entirely out of keeping with their personalities. In the Civil War question above, some students might try to show off by writing, "One may conclude, after exhaustive study of the cogent data on this issue, that there are three different yet interrelated causes that eventually led to that bloody strife called the Civil War." Chances are you have already put the teacher to sleep. Write naturally. Be yourself. Remember that you are a unique person.

Just as inappropriate as overwriting is mixing current slang with formal English. The effect on the reader can be jarring and laughable, as in this excerpt from a student essay: "Odysseus had been warned by the gods that he would be punished if any of the cattle on the island were disturbed. Yet his men were so hungry that they killed some of the cattle and pigged out on the meat." *Pigging out* may be suitable in the school cafeteria, but it is certainly not suitable in a discussion of the *Odyssey*.

6. *Lack of design*

Papers that ramble aimlessly are usually the result of a student not planning a design ahead of time. Even if the teacher does not require one, write an outline. Use proper outline form (see pages 138–139) and be certain to use specific examples throughout. (See also points 2, 3, and 4 above.) When writing your outline, write the main topics first and then fill in the subtopics. (See examples on pages 137–138.) [Using a computer makes writing an outline relatively easy.]

Here is a sample outline of the title and main topics of this chapter:

Step 1.

SIX COMMON PROBLEMS IN WRITING
AND HOW TO DEAL WITH THEM [TITLE]

I.   Writing block

II.   Writing poor introductions and conclusions

III. Weak opening sentences

IV.   Straying from the topic

V.   Inappropriate style

VI.   Lack of design

Step 2.

Now go back and fill in the subtopics, as in this example:

SIX COMMON PROBLEMS IN WRITING
AND HOW TO DEAL WITH THEM [TITLE]

I.   Writing block
   A.   Think through topic
   B.   Jot thoughts randomly
   C.   Make outline
   D.   Take a break
   E.   Write final paragraph
   F.   Skip ahead

II.   Writing poor introductions and conclusions
   A.   Requirements: introductory paragraph
   B.   Requirements: concluding paragraph
   C.   Suggested techniques
      1.   Write introduction last
      2.   Write conclusion first

III.   Weak opening sentences
   A.   Rule: repeat part of question
   B.   Example: Civil War question
   C.   Longer essays
      1.   Main idea opening sentence
      2.   Essential information first paragraph
   D.   Example: *Winnie the Pooh*

IV.   Straying from the topic
   A.   Keep main idea in mind
   B.   Repeat key words in topic sentences

V.   Inappropriate style
   A.   To impress teacher
   B.   Example: Civil War question
   C.   Avoid slang

VI.   Lack of design
   A.   Outline: main topics
   B.   Outline: subtopics

6 Six Ways to Increase Your Vocabulary

Having a good working vocabulary is an indispensable tool for all students. If they cannot express themselves accurately and clearly, students cannot look forward to success in subjects that demand articulation of ideas.

Here are some suggestions for increasing your vocabulary:

- Buy a "How to Increase Your Vocabulary" book and use it at least once a day for fifteen minutes or more. [Buy a vocabulary-building program for your computer at a software store and use it every day.]

- Read. Read anything and everything: menus, posters, books, magazines, newspapers, *the dictionary,* signs, billboards, anything. Frequent exposure to the printed word will help build your working vocabulary.

- Learn to identify meanings of words from context. For example, in the sentence, *The nefarious thief . . . ,* the adjective *nefarious* coupled with the noun *thief* probably means that the fellow was not up to any good. In fact, *nefarious* means *evil.* Sometimes the context will be of no help: *She listened to the* vapid *conversation around her.* If you think *vapid* means *rapid, interesting, loud,* or *soft,* you would be wrong: It means *dull* or *lifeless.* In such cases, use a dictionary.

- Buy a paperback thesaurus and use it. A thesaurus lists words with similar meanings (synonyms).

- Use a dictionary any time you see or hear a new word.

- Listen carefully to teachers and other adults; question them when they use words you do not know.

7 How to Use the Computer to Improve Your Grades

Increasingly, computers are being used by students in school and colleges for a number of tasks. This chapter, however, will focus only on ways you can use the computer to improve yourself at school.

- **To improve subjects that require longer papers.** Learn to type if you have not already done so. Typing is faster than hand-writing—and more accurate. Software stores carry typing programs that you can use to teach yourself to type.

- **To improve individual subjects.** Software stores carry programs designed to increase your competence in a number of subjects: vocabulary, spelling, writing, mathematics, history, and geography, to name a few.

- **To improve the writing of your essays.** Software stores carry grammar-checks that will proofread your writing, show you your mistakes, and let you correct them. Be careful: Grammar-checks have no sense of style. (See page 136: "Inappropriate style."]

  CAUTION: Some schools and teachers may not permit students to use grammar-checks and consider their use a form of cheating.

- **To improve the spelling in your written work.** Word processors and even some electronic typewriters now have spell-checks. Be careful: Spell-checks will not catch the differences between words such as *two* and *too,* and *from* and *form,* so proofread your papers carefully.

  CAUTION: Some schools and teachers may not permit students to use spell-checks and consider their use a form of cheating.

- **To improve retention.** Computers can be used to drill yourself for material you must memorize. (See pages 102–104.)

- **To keep accurate notes.** Typed notes are invariably more accurate, neater, and faster to write than are those that are handwritten.

- **To give neatness and order to your essays and longer papers.** Using a computer for themes and longer papers is becoming increasingly common in many schools and colleges and, in fact, has become a requirement in many schools. However, when typing formal papers, use Standard Manuscript Format for proper margins and spacing. (See page 142.)

Three words of caution regarding computer use:

1. Writing becomes so easy and so fast on a computer that many students find themselves writing too much. So, when you proofread your final draft, cut out all unnecessary words, sentences, and even paragraphs.

2. Always use a backup system when writing important papers or copying notes. Electricity does have a way of going off from time to time, and there is no measuring the distress when little brothers or sisters accidentally erase an entire paper of an older sibling.

3. When writing a research paper, be careful not to plagiarize (that is, to use an author's words as your own). Computers make it easy to save an author's words, phrases, sentences, and ideas. When typing an author's words into your computer, use quotation marks or an asterisk (*) or some other system to indicate those words or ideas that are not yours. When you are typing your paper, be careful to avoid using these words or ideas unless you use footnotes.

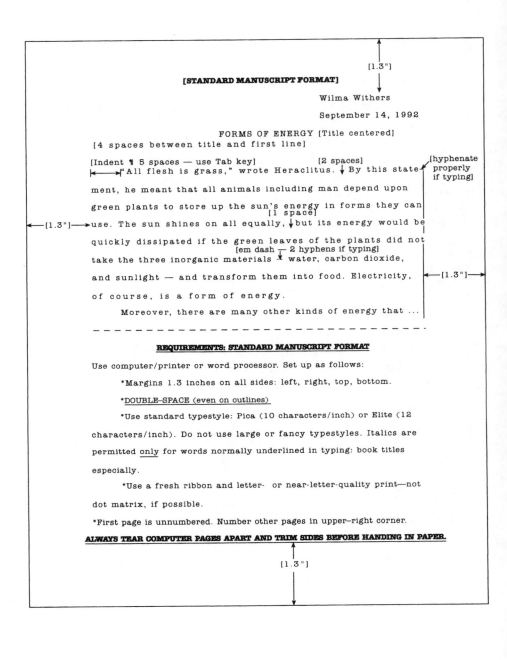

[1.3"]

[STANDARD MANUSCRIPT FORMAT]

Wilma Withers

September 14, 1992

FORMS OF ENERGY [Title centered]
[4 spaces between title and first line]

[Indent ¶ 5 spaces — use Tab key]   [2 spaces]   [hyphenate
"All flesh is grass," wrote Heraclitus. By this state-   properly
                                                           if typing]
ment, he meant that all animals including man depend upon

green plants to store up the sun's energy in forms they can
                                  [1 space]
[1.3"] use. The sun shines on all equally, but its energy would be

quickly dissipated if the green leaves of the plants did not
                              [em dash — 2 hyphens if typing]
take the three inorganic materials — water, carbon dioxide,

and sunlight — and transform them into food. Electricity,   [1.3"]

of course, is a form of energy.

        Moreover, there are many other kinds of energy that ...

REQUIREMENTS: STANDARD MANUSCRIPT FORMAT

Use computer/printer or word processor. Set up as follows:

        *Margins 1.3 inches on all sides: left, right, top, bottom.

        *DOUBLE–SPACE (even on outlines)

        *Use standard typestyle: Pica (10 characters/inch) or Elite (12

characters/inch). Do not use large or fancy typestyles. Italics are

permitted only for words normally underlined in typing: book titles

especially.

        *Use a fresh ribbon and letter- or near-letter-quality print—not

dot matrix, if possible.

*First page is unnumbered. Number other pages in upper–right corner.

ALWAYS TEAR COMPUTER PAGES APART AND TRIM SIDES BEFORE HANDING IN PAPER.

[1.3"]

UNIT IX

The next best thing to knowing
something is knowing where
to find it.

Samuel Johnson

THE LIBRARY

1 Three Ways to Use the School Library to Help Your Day-to-Day Schoolwork

Many students do not realize how useful libraries can be in improving their day-to-day schoolwork. The library is too often used as a place where one can go and have a pleasant social chat, or as a place one *has* to go to work on an assigned research paper.

Moreover, students frequently are not aware that they have two libraries at their disposal: the school library and the public library. It is useful to have a card for the public library in case the school library does not meet your needs.

Since the school library is the most convenient source for most students, the following suggestions for improving your course work are based on that facility:

1. Take a half hour or so to browse through the various sections of the school library, noting especially the kinds of books in the reference area:

   - Note particularly the various encyclopedias on the subjects in which you are interested or in which you are having problems. School libraries usually carry special encyclopedias on the subjects you are studying: literature, history, sciences, math, languages, etc.

   - Note, too, the sections that have *pictorial* accounts of subjects in which you are having difficulty.

   - Find out what tapes, microfilm, videocassettes, picture files, and other renderings of subjects are available in addition to books. Ask the librarian for help if you do not already know how to use these aids.

   - Check to see the kinds of magazines and periodicals the library subscribes to or has files on. Magazines such as *American Heritage, Scientific American,* and others that specialize in a particular field can be a source of support for your studies.

- [Check to see what kinds of computer aids are available: computer catalogs, computer periodical indexes, or computers that can access information from other libraries.]

2. Zero in on courses in which you are having problems.

   - Ask the librarian for clear, simple, and readable books on subjects that trouble you.

   - Find popular versions of such subjects that are readable but also written by reputable scholars.

   - Read plot summaries of plays, novels, etc., that you are having difficulty understanding.

     CAUTION: Such summaries give only the barest outlines of a work. Never read a summary *in place of* the assigned book, only as an aid to understanding.

   - Listen to tapes to help you with difficult material. Some school libraries have tapes that are useful for drilling yourself in languages, and even in spelling. In addition, there may be compact discs or tapes of readings from short stories, plays, and poetry.

3. [Some school libraries now have computers and software available for student use. Ask the librarian what is available in your difficult subject, and schedule time in the library to use the program that best suits your needs.]

2 Useful Information that Reference Books Provide

Reference books serve two functions: They supply basic facts in various fields, and they refer you to other books that have the information you seek. Know where the reference section is located in your school library.

Here is a list of the reference books that can be found in most school libraries:

Dictionary. This reference book is often thought of as giving only the definitions of words. However, it supplies a lot more information: origins of words, pronunciations, and sometimes supplements in the back of the book. Such supplements might include guides to punctuation, information on manuscript form, tables of weights and measures, and special signs and symbols.

Use (or buy) a recent dictionary because technological change is moving so fast. For example, a 1980 dictionary does not even list *compact disc.*

Thesaurus. A thesaurus is a collection of synonyms and antonyms. That is, words are classified by their similar and dissimilar meanings. For example, *laugh* as a verb: *snicker, snigger, titter, giggle, cackle, chortle, chuckle, guffaw, howl, scream, roar, shriek,* etc. Antonyms: *weep, cry, mope.* (Owning your own paperback thesaurus can be very convenient.)

Encyclopedia. There are two kinds: general and special. General encyclopedias such as the *Britannica* supply information on all subjects and fields. Special encyclopedias deal in specialized fields such as art, history, religion, etc.

Atlas. An atlas is a collection of maps. It may be a world atlas giving maps of the geography of the world today. Or it may be a historical atlas, say, of American history, ancient history, modern European history, etc.

Almanac. An almanac is published annually and gives information on people, events, places, etc., that were important during that year. A popular almanac is the *World Almanac.*

Biography. There are a number of different types of biographies, which are accounts of the lives and accomplishments of people. An *autobiography* was written by a particular person about his or her own life. A *biography* was written by one person about another person's life. A *biographical dictionary* gives accounts of people according to whether they are living or dead, how prominent they were in their fields, or by their nationality. *Who's Who in America,* for example, gives biographical information on prominent living Americans. *Who Was Who in America* gives biographical data on prominent deceased Americans.

Readers' Guide to Periodical Literature. This reference work is discussed on pages 157–158.

7 How the Dewey Decimal System Works

Melvil Dewey was a man of enormous energy and imagination—and he had a passion for order. He was especially appalled by the disorder of books he saw in American libraries, which made it difficult for him to find the book he wanted. When he arrived at Amherst College in 1874, he developed a system of classifying books. Moreover, when Dewey died, he left part of his estate to perpetuating and perfecting his system. This is the chief reason that so many libraries today use the Dewey decimal system.

Dewey set up his system this way:

Fiction. Novels are shelved alphabetically by the author's last name. (Short-story collections are often shelved near the fiction section, with the designation *SC*. They are arranged alphabetically by the last name of the author or the editor. They may also be shelved in the fiction section. Check with the librarian.)

Nonfiction. The rest of the library is an arrangement of nonfiction by general subject classes. Here are the ten main classes in the Dewey system:

000	Generalities
100	Philosophy & related disciplines
200	Religion
300	Social sciences
400	Language
500	Pure sciences
600	Technology (Applied sciences)
700	The arts
800	Literature
900	General geography & history

Within each division is a further division that is characterized by decimals (hence, the Dewey *decimal* system). For example, the numerical division of the history of the United States is 973. This number is subdivided by decimals according to their historical occurrence:

U.S. history—Colonial	973.2
U.S. history—Revolution	973.3
U.S. history—1787–1799	973.4
U.S. history—19th century	973.5

[When using the computer catalog, you may not use the abbreviation *U.S.* Instead you must type the entire designation:
UNITED STATES HISTORY COLONIAL
after pressing the Subject key.]

The Library of Congress system. The largest library in the world, the Library of Congress in Washington, D.C., uses its own system of classification. Since it is normally not used in school libraries, or in many public libraries, you need not know how it operates.

4 How to Find What You Need in the Library

Most school libraries and many public libraries use the Dewey decimal classification system (see pages 149–150). This system is easy to use if you know the system and how to use it. [See page 152 for libraries with computer catalogs.]

Call number. Each book has been given a letter or number designation that appears in two places: on the spine of the shelved book and on its cards in the card catalog.

Card catalog. The card catalog tells you four essential pieces of information about each book: its author, its title, its subject, and its call number.

Here is an example of a typical card:

940.54	Crusade in Europe.
Eisen	Eisenhower, Dwight David, 1890–1969.
	Crusade in Europe . . . New York, Holt,
	1949.
	563p.

A nonfiction book such as the one above would appear in at least three different places in the card catalog:

In the *C*s for the first word in the title: *Crusade.*

In the *E*s for the first letter of the author's last name: *Eisenhower.*

Under the subject heading: *World War, 1939–1945.*

To find this book, simply write down its call number (940.54 Eisen) on a slip of paper, along with the name of the author and the title. Then go to that section of the library that shelves the 940s, and locate your book by the call number on its spine.

Occasionally, a subject card will refer you to another subject card. This is called a cross-reference, and the card will have *See* or *See also* printed on it.

Here are examples of cross-reference cards:

	WORLD WAR II
	See
	WORLD WAR, 1939–1945

	AIRPLANES
	See also
	AERONAUTICS

Libraries with Computer Catalogs. Increasingly, libraries are using computer catalogs to help readers find what they need. These computers are faster, more convenient, and more helpful than traditional card catalogs.

A typical computer catalog monitor might display the following information on its screen:

Author

Title

Subject

Words in title

The easiest way to find your call number is to know and type in either the title or the last name of the author of the book you need.

If you cannot remember either, you can call up the names of authors and the titles of all books in the library on that subject (*World War 1939–1945,* for example). However, larger libraries may have hundreds of titles under that subject, thereby complicating your job enormously.

If, on the other hand, you can remember that *Europe* or *Crusade* was in the title, you can bring up all books with that word in the title after you have selected *Words in title.* Then you can find the title of the book you are looking for: *Crusade in Europe.*

When you have brought up your book's "card" on the screen, it will supply the same information (and possibly more) as a card from a noncomputerized system.

Fiction. Novels are all shelved alphabetically by author and have no Dewey number. Often, libraries designate fiction by *F* or *FI* above the first letters of the author's last name. Moreover, fiction books are likely to have only two cards in the card catalog: one for author, another for title. (Some libraries are also beginning to list fiction under subject: *World War, 1939–1945,* for example.)

If, then, you know the last name of the author of the book you are looking for, you have no need to go to the card catalog. Simply go to the fiction shelf, find three or more letters of the author's name on the spine of the book, and take it out.

If you know only the title, you must first look up the title in the card catalog, find out the author's name, and then locate the book.

Short-story collections are usually shelved near the fiction and generally carry the designation *SC.* They may also be shelved in the fiction section. They are listed in the card catalog by the author's last name or by the editor's last name.

[Computer catalogs having *Words in title* will list fiction books as well as nonfiction.]

Narrowing a subject. Computerized catalogs can easily be used to focus on a subject you are interested in. Suppose, for example, you are interested in exploring the role of women in medieval England. Here is what you can do:

1. First punch the Subject key and type in *women*. This might bring up *Women—see related subjects.*

2. Then go back to Subject and type in *Women—medieval.* This might bring up three books, including one that looks interesting: *Women in a Medieval City.*

3. If you bring that title up on your monitor, it will also list related topics: *Women—history—Middle ages* and *Women—Europe—social conditions.*

4. Keep narrowing your subject until you have just the titles of the books you need.

Tapes, videocassettes, compact discs, and other audiovisual aids. These, too, appear in the catalog, usually by subject. Here is an example of the card for an audiocassette (tape):

```
AC
782.b       Gershwin, George, 1898–1937
G           Porgy and Bess
```

[Computer catalogs list audiovisual aids in the same way that books are listed: author, title, subject, words in title.]

Since material of this kind is often housed apart from the books, ask the librarian for help in finding where such material is kept.

Magazines and periodicals. Much useful information, particularly for research projects, appears in magazines and periodicals. Because of space limitations, many school libraries keep only a small number of back issues of magazines, and only a few titles as well. Some school libraries, however, do have microfiche copies of some magazines and of important periodicals such as *The New York Times.*

Two important printed indexes for current literature are *The New York Times Index* and *The Readers' Guide to Periodical Literature* (see page 157). There are other specialized indexes as well, usually in larger libraries:

General Science Index

Art Index

Applied Science & Technology Index

[Larger libraries also have computerized periodical and newspaper indexes that specialize in material printed during the last three to seven years (when such services became available). To use a computer index, you simply type in the subject, and the references will be printed out (see next page).]

InfoTrac - General Periodical Index-P ~ 1985 - June 1992

Heading: OLYMPIC ATHLETES
            -United States

1.   Women of mettle. (women win 9 of 11 U.S.
medals) (1992 Winter Olympics) by E.M. Swift il v76
Sports Illustrated March 2 '92 p38(2)
        ABSTRACT & TEXT AVAILABLE

2.   All in the family; Griffith Joyner and Joyner-
Kersee sizzle in Seoul. (Florence Griffith Joyner;
Jackie Joyner-Kersee) by Pete Axthelm il V112 Newsweek
Oct 10 '88 p58(4)
        46J0199   40Y0737

InfoTrac - National Newspaper Index ~ 1989 - June 1992

Heading: OLYMPIC ATHLETES
            -Commemorative coins, stamps, etc.

1.   Five Olympic athletes and their brief biographies
will be featured in a new commemorative series.
(includes other stamp collecting information)
(Pastimes pages) (column) by Barth Healey il 16 col
in. v139 The New York Times June 17 '90 sec 1 p22(N)
p52(L) col 1

2.   And the winners are four movie classics and five
Olympic champions. (U.S. Postal Service, new stamp
issues) (column) by Barth Healey il 10 col in. v139
The New York Times March 11 '90 sec 1 p20(N) p59(L)
col 1

InfoTrac - General Periodical Index-P ~ 1985 - June 1992

Heading: OLYMPIC ATHLETES
            -Commemorative coins, stamps, etc.

1.   American Olympians. (postage stamps) il v231
Stamps June 16 '90 p389(1)
        55D6122

2.   Jesse Owens stamp design unveiled. il v230 Stamps
March 10 '90 p357(1)
        53K6096

Readers' Guide to Periodical Literature. This reference book is an indispensable guide to anyone who needs a magazine or a periodical. Unlike the card catalog, the listings in the *Readers' Guide* are by author and by subject, but not by title of the article.

The *Readers' Guide* does not carry an index to *all* magazines, but it does cover more than a hundred popular American magazines in a variety of fields.

Here is an excerpt from the *Readers' Guide:*

GIRLS
　　See also
　　Sex differences
GIRLS' CLUBS
　　See also
　　Boys & Girls Clubs of America
GIS *See* Geographic information systems
GIVENS, CHARLES J.
　　　　about
　　The guru of getting rich quick. P. McCarthy. *World Press Review* 39:38-9 Ja '92
GIVING
　　The empathy factor: when people have less, they often give more. E Salholz. il *Newsweek* 119:23 Ja 13 '92
GLANDS
　　See also
　　Prostate gland
GLASS
　　See also
　　Glassware
　　Windows
GLASS CLEANERS *See* Cleaning compositions
GLASSWARE
　　　　Collectors and collecting
　　Greentown glass. G. Michael. il *Antiques & Collecting Hobbies* 96:31 Ja '92
GLEN CANYON DAM (ARIZ.)
　　Saving the flows [water flow regulations] G. Randall. il *Audubon* 94:96-9 Ja/F '92
GLOBAL NAVIGATION SATELLITE SYSTEM *See* Glonass (Global Navigation Satellite System)
GLOBAL POSITIONING SYSTEM
　　Air Transport Assn. hopes evolving technology will end need for MLS [GPS/Glonass receivers as alternative to microwave landing systems] P. J. Klass. *Aviation Week & Space Technology* 136:40 Ja 20 '92
　　FAA says GPS lacks accuracy needed for precision approaches. B. D. Nordwall. il *Aviation Week & Space Technology* 136:50-1 Ja 20 '92
GLOBAL WARMING *See* Greenhouse effect
GLOBULAR CLUSTERS *See* Stars—Clusters
GLONASS (GLOBAL NAVIGATION SATELLITE SYSTEM)
　　Air Transport Assn. hopes evolving technology will end need for MLS [GPS/Glonass receivers as alternative to microwave landing systems] P. J. Klass. *Aviation Week & Space Technology* 136:40 Ja 20 '92
GM *See* General Motors Corp.
GNP *See* Gross national product
GOD
　　See also
　　Jesus Christ
　　Monotheism
　　Trinity
GODZILLA (FICTIONAL CHARACTER)
　　Leaping lizard [alleged America bashing in motion picture Godzilla vs. King Ghidora] J. Impoco. il *U.S. News & World Report* 112:17 Ja 13 '92
GODZILLA VS. KING GHIDORA [film] See Motion picture reviews—Single works
GOING PUBLIC (SECURITIES) *See* Initial public offerings (Securities)

Here is an entry:

GODZILLA (FICTIONAL CHARACTER)
Leaping lizard [alleged America bashing in motion picture
Godzilla vs. King Ghidora] J. Impoco. il *U.S. News
& World Report* 112:17 Ja 13 '92

Here is the translation of the above entry: The title of the article
is "Leaping Lizard," the main idea is the supposed put-down of
America in the movie *Godzilla vs. King Ghidora,* the author is J.
Impoco, the article is illustrated and appeared in *U.S. News &
World Report,* volume 112, page 17, and the issue of the magazine is
January 13, 1992.

Appendixes

TO THE TEACHER OR ADVISOR

Appendix I

Dealing with Students' Frustrations

Nothing is more destructive to the studying process than constant frustration. In the short run, frustration inhibits the problem-solving process. In the long run, it leads to an "I give up" attitude.

When students become frustrated, it is always well to remind them that they have the innate ability to solve their problems and that thousands of people like them have worked their way through the same types of problems.

It is well to emphasize, too, that there is nothing *wrong* with students who are frustrated by studying. They probably have not yet focused on the best approach.

Study problems are best solved by the advisor and the student stepping back from the situation, looking at the problems objectively, and then *finding new approaches that work.*

This book is organized so that students can use the table-of-contents pages to identify their problems quickly and go to work immediately on the new approaches.

But they need the advisor's help. The spirit may be willing, but the flesh is often weak. You can help students most by being patient, understanding, and persistent. Even the suggested easy methods at the beginning of each unit take time to put into practice.

Setting reasonable, attainable goals and using a reward system will go a long way toward helping a student cope with frustrations.

Turn to Appendix II to help students identify their study problems.

Appendix II

Identifying General Study Problems

The questions below are provided as a preliminary diagnosis of general study problems. The questions are divided into three steps:

1. Identifying the problems

2. Finding solutions

3. Following through on solutions

It is suggested that you make notations and, if you wish, make copies of these pages and keep them in a file.

Identifying the problems

What are the student's chief problems?

What is the major cause of the problems?

Is there more than one cause? What are they?

Has the problem gotten worse recently? Why?

Has the problem improved recently? Why?

Is the problem long-term or recent?

Has the student complicated the problem? Why?

NOTE: If you suspect that the student has a learning disability, turn to Appendix IV, pages 167–168.

Finding solutions

What could the student try that has not been tried yet?

What are the student's strong points? How can they be used to study better?

What solutions can you each think of?

What shortcuts can be taken?

How can the student's problems be simplified?

Can the problem be simplified by breaking it into smaller and more manageable pieces? How?

[Would learning to use a computer help?]

Following through on solutions

What did the student try that worked?

Will it work in other subjects?

What did the student try that failed? Why?

Did the student work every day at trying to solve the problems? Why not?

To focus on more-specific study problems, ask the student to take the Diagnostic Test on pages 11–13. Review together the results of the test, and then begin to work on specific problems using the recommended pages.

If you are a classroom teacher needing a methodical approach to use with your students, turn to Appendix III, pages 164–166.

Appendix III

Using This Book Effectively in the Classroom

Teachers can use *How to Study* effectively in the classroom. One specific approach that has been in use for over five years is given below.

This approach focuses on a six-session method (one session a week) and concentrates on:

- introducing the book in the classroom (first session)

- using the book over five consecutive weeks

- defining areas of continuing responsibility for parents and students

Introducing the book in the classroom (first session)

- Students become familiar with the book through an examination of the table of contents (pages vii–ix). Class focus will be on units to be studied over the next five weeks, for example, Units II, III, IV, VI, and VII.

- Students are shown the purpose and relevance of the book, first to assess their own study skills and then to choose goals for improvement in the unit under examination.

- Students are instructed to set goals for themselves that are:

  - achievable (really within their reach)

  - believable (known by the student to be achievable)

  - observable (can be seen and measured by the student and the teacher)

- Students take the self-test on pages 11–13. The results of this test will not be seen by anyone else, so students are told to answer *honestly*.

- Students refer to page 16 for the results of their self-test. The teacher asks students to note in pencil which units they need to give special attention to, as indicated by the *NO* responses.

- Students choose the first goal for the next week and are asked to read Unit I, Chapters 6 and 7, for the next session.

Using the book in five subsequent sessions. Assume that the following units are to be assigned over the next five weeks: II, III, IV, VI, and VII. The general plan for each session would go something like this:

- The teacher first introduces the unit by reading selected passages. (For older students, reading a unit might be given as a homework assignment.) Students follow along, highlighting pertinent information for rereading and later discussion. Students are reminded of their need to set a goal and to devise specific ways suggested by the text to move toward meeting that goal.

- Students go back and focus on the chapters that best suit their needs. They write out their goal for the week and then specify several ways they will try to meet that goal.

- The teacher will move from student to student during this writing process to make certain that the goals and means chosen are *achievable, believable,* and *observable.*

- Students will open their notebooks every day during the *How to Study* weeks and note precisely what steps they have taken to achieve their goals—and how well their steps are working.

- The teacher can encourage class discussions on what techniques worked for whom, and why.

Defining areas of continuing responsibility for parents and students. With day-school students who are younger (grades 6 or 7, for example), getting parental cooperation can be very helpful.

On the next page is a copy of a letter than can be sent to day-school parents, clearly indicating the areas of parent and student responsibility after the completion of a six-week course.

Dear Parents:

We have completed the *How to Study* series with your child and have had a study-skills discussion series with all new older students. Here are some highlights from the course and some suggestions for parent facilitation of homework. Please talk these over with your child.

Student's area of responsibility:

1. To know that when grades are improving, study skills are working.

2. To know that when grades are going down, study skills need to be changed and made more effective.

3. To take charge of one's own progress through:

   a. organizing a daily time schedule, setting a firm time to start and a good estimated time to finish;

   b. keeping an accurate assignment sheet and meeting deadlines daily;

   c. improving concentration by removing distractions (no radio, TV, phone interferences);

   d. preparing for tests well ahead to avoid cramming and sleepless nights;

   e. avoiding careless mistakes by taking time to check over work and tests and by organizing materials for the day.

4. To make a commitment to completing all homework. Try the open-door policy, which makes a "public" declaration at home that the student is indeed studying and is willing to be checked on without being interrupted.

Parents' area of cooperation:

1. To provide a quiet, adequately appointed place for the student to study;

2. To give support, encouragement, and understanding of the real homework demands on students—about thirty minutes of work per night per academic subject. To help the student select a reasonable study schedule;

3. To cooperate in making study time a quiet time(controlling distractions);

4. To encourage the student to attend to his or her balanced needs for nutrition, exercise, sleep.

School's responsibility:

1. To teach and evaluate fairly;

2. To assist students in understanding their individual aptitude/achievement level and facilitate their academic goals.

Sincerely,

Appendix IV

Common Learning Problems and Suggested Ways to Deal with Them

Dyslexia. This is a learning disorder in which the brain has difficulty decoding words and their sounds.

Symptoms: difficulty in sounding out words, poor spelling, cramped or illegible handwriting, slow reading rate, and poor comprehension.

Recommendation: Have the student tested by a reading diagnostician. Consult with the parents, if you think it advisable. After the diagnosis, the usual treatment is tutoring with a reading specialist.

Remarks: This disorder is a common reading problem. Apparently it cannot be cured, but it can be remediated. Dyslexics often succeed in visual fields like architecture, design, and art. Famous dyslexics include Leonardo da Vinci and Winston Churchill.

Mixed dominance. This is another common reading problem, particularly among younger children. A right-handed person should be right-eyed (that is, the right eye should be the stronger, more dominant when the student reads), and a left-handed person should be left-eyed. Mixed dominance occurs when a right-handed person has a dominant left eye, or vice versa.

Symptoms: poor reading and writing ability, manifesting itself prominently in reversal of letters (*d* for *b, p* for *q*) and reversal of words (*saw* for *was*).

Recommendation: As with dyslexia, have the student tested by a reading diagnostician. Tutoring with a specialist may be called for.

Hearing/vision problems. Students who do poorly in school sometimes have a simple hearing or vision problem.

Recommendation: If you suspect that a student has one of these problems, have him or her tested by a specialist, with the consent of the parents, if needed. Often the solution to a vision problem is simply a pair of glasses. Students who have hearing problems should be seated in the front of every class they attend.

Attention-deficit disorder (ADD). Children with ADD (chiefly boys) have both behavioral and educational problems. The causes—and indeed the very existence—of the disorder are subjects of intense debate in the medical community.

Symptoms: inattentiveness, restlessness (even hyperactivity), lack of concentration, impulsiveness, talking excessively, disinclination to finish tasks, tendency to be easily distracted, and difficulty in following directions.

Recommendation: Have the child tested by a specialist, with the parents' consent, if needed. Treatment for the child may include medication, behavior modification, or specialized schooling.